The

BOY'S BODY BOOK

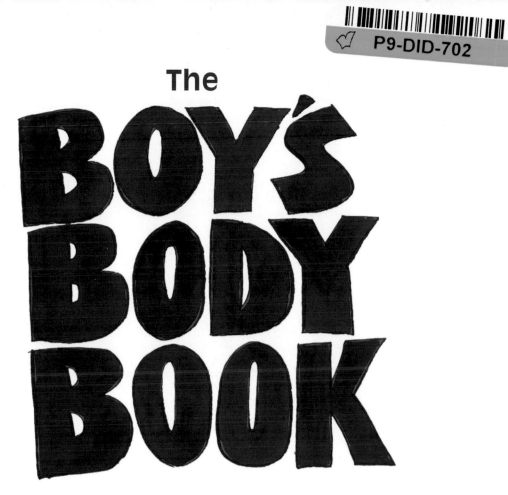

By Kelli Dunham, RN
Illustrated by Steve Bjorkman

APPLESAUCE PRESS

KENNEBUNKPORT, MAINE

13-Digit ISBN: 978-1-60433-832-4
10-Digit ISBN: 1-60433-832-6

This book may be ordered by mail from the publisher. Please include $5.99 for postage and handling.
Please support your local bookseller first!

Books published by Cider Mill Press Book Publishers are available at special discounts for bulk purchases in the United States by corporations, institutions, and other organizations. For more information, please contact the publisher.

Applesauce Press is an imprint of
Cider Mill Press Book Publishers
"Where good books are ready for press"
PO Box 454
12 Spring Street
Kennebunkport, Maine 04046

Visit us on the Web!
www.cidermillpress.com

Typography: Antique Olive, Berthold Akzidenz Grotesk, Bolten, Century Schoolbook,
Frutiger, Gill Sans, Glypha, Imperfect, Monotype Sorts, Sue Ellen Francisco

Printed in China
2 3 4 5 6 7 8 9 0

TABLE OF CONTENTS

DESTINY IS A MATTER OF CHOICE

By Robert Anastas, Founder of SADD (Students Against Driving Drunk)

As an educator, I fully endorse and recommend *The Boy's Body Book*. Kelli Dunham presents important material in a very easy-to-understand and factual manner. In my travels speaking to students throughout the world, I have found they need a solid foundation of facts to make proper decisions. A young person's destiny is not a matter of chance; it is a matter of choice.

I have spent over 30 years working with young people in schools and colleges. My major focus as an educator and counselor has been on illegal drinking and drug abuse. Over the years I began to see a society whose young people were exposed to a great deal of peer pressure to go along with the crowd. Despite the valiant efforts of many in the field of drug and alcohol prevention, abuse continued to soar during the 1980s and early '90s. It seemed clear that teenagers were going to do "their thing" no matter what we said. I am convinced that a great deal of illegal drinking and drug abuse is caused by peer pressure, and with this in mind I created SADD (Students Against Driving Drunk). I found through my work at SADD that because the problem of illegal drinking and the use of illegal drugs lies with young people that the solution lies with them as well. In order to solve a problem of this magnitude, we must first shed a light on it, and then look at the root cause. Through my experience working with teenagers, I concluded that deaths caused by drinking and driving had been camouflaged for teenagers in two ways. First, lack of communication between parents and their children, and second, the peer pressure that teenagers face every day doing things they may not wish to do. My experience led me to believe that, as determined as we are to provide a drug-free environment for our children, statistics have proven that our efforts have fallen on deaf ears. My belief is that if we give our sons information that is designed to address the broader subjects of responsible decision-making based on factual information, they will make the proper choices. They must be equipped with information to address the symptoms of high-risk behavior with key life skills (i.e., self-esteem, motivation, maturity, and leadership).

This book presents good information on a wide range of topics that will help young men make proper choices on their journey through life. It is my wish that all boys reading this book will get a better understanding of their bodies and how to deal with the many pressures associated with adolescence and thereby gain a head start on a productive life. Parents of preteens can feel confident that this book will allow their children to find the answers to the many questions that arise concerning their development. It may also open the door to healthy conversations between you as parents and your children.

WHAT'S CHANGING?

AT THIS TIME in your life, on some days it might seem like everything is changing!

Your **body** is changing.

Your **feelings** are changing.

Your **relationships** with your friends and family members are changing.

It hardly seems fair, does it?

Especially because as a boy gets older, he often finds that it gets more difficult to talk with the adults in his life about the kinds of things he used to. There are a few very good reasons for this:

● He might be afraid to ask a question he thinks he should already know the answer to.

● He might feel like he doesn't know the best (or the most polite) word to use to describe something that is happening with his body.

● He might be worried that something he is feeling isn't normal, and that people would laugh at him if they knew what was going on in his head (or his body).

This is not fun, but it is 100 percent normal!

And it isn't just kids who sometimes develop troubles communicating. You may have noticed that sometimes the adults around you have trouble talking about the changes you are going through. It seems like they should be able to handle it, since they've been through the "kid-to-adult" transition themselves. So what are they worried about? Mostly the same things you are! They might worry about not having all the right information. They might remember how awkward this time was for them and feel like they don't have any advice to help you get through it. They might even be worried (does this sound familiar?) about not knowing the correct or polite terms for body parts and body processes, what words you might use, or what information you might already have learned from your friends or by looking around online. And they might be especially worried about giving you more information than you want to know or are ready for.

With boys and adults all red-faced

and stammering and stuttering, it makes it hard for information to flow back and forth. That's where this book comes in.

This book has a lot of information about the changes that are coming your way. We hope it will answer many of your questions so that you feel ready and informed, not confused and scared.

There is no right or wrong way to use this book. You are the expert on how to make it work best for you! You might want to sit right down and read it from cover to cover all at once (maybe under the covers with a flashlight, if you are feeling particularly shy). You might just look at the chapters that interest you for now, and then put it on your shelf until you have more questions about the other stuff in the rest of the book. If you aren't interested or don't want to know about the stuff in this book, no problem. You can always put this book away until later when you want to know more!

This is just one small

book, so it can't contain the answers for every question that you might have about this exciting—but sometimes confusing—time of your life. Having a trusted adult that you can talk to comes in handy. If something written here doesn't make sense to you, or is different from your experience, discuss it with a parent, teacher, health care provider, or another responsible, trusted grown-up.

Although this time is not easy, you already have many resources for dealing with the changes that are coming your way. You have past experiences that you have learned from, you have friends that are going through the same things you are, and you have adults who care about you. All these things will help make the process smoother. Best of luck to you as you begin the important transition of growing from a boy into a man.

BOYS SAY:

I FOUND IT KIND OF EMBARRASSING TO TALK TO PEOPLE ABOUT MY BODY, SO I WAS GLAD THERE WAS A BOOK LIKE THIS ONE. I USED TO KEEP MINE HIDDEN IN MY SOCK DRAWER WHERE NO ONE WOULD LOOK FOR IT.

-Danny, age 15

Chapter 1:

WHAT ON EARTH IS GOING ON AROUND HERE?

If you are a boy between the ages of 8 and 12, you have probably noticed some changes in your body. These changes are called puberty. Puberty is the general name for the process everyone goes through to change from a kid to an adult. Some of the changes are physical, and some of the changes are emotional.

Puberty takes place over several years, and while it may seem like the process will never end, most boys are through puberty by age 16 or 17.

All About This Thing Called Puberty

The changes your body will go through can seem a bit mysterious, but they basically come from one thing: extra amounts of special chemicals (called hormones) being

produced in your body. In boys, the hormone most responsible for puberty is called testosterone, while the one responsible for puberty in girls is called estrogen. You'll be hearing a lot more about testosterone in the pages ahead.

Growth Spurts

One of the first changes you might notice is that you are growing quickly. During this rapid growth spurt, some boys find that clothes that fit at the beginning of the school year are too small by Halloween! Soon, your shoulders will start to get wider and your muscles will start to develop more.

This can make you feel sore, since your muscles don't grow as fast as your bones do. Heating pads can help with some of the pain, as can exercising. Some boys get their growth spurt early, while others don't get theirs until later. This is called being an early or late bloomer. Don't worry if you are the shortest one in your class, or if you feel like you'll never stop growing. Your body will grow until it's the perfect height for you.

One kind of annoying (and possibly embarrassing) part of the rapid increase in size and height is that your arms, legs, hands, and feet may grow faster than the rest of your body. So while the rest of your body is catching up, you might feel a little (or more than a little) clumsy. Sooner or later, your body will once again be all the same size and you'll be back to your smooth self.

Whoa, What's Going on Down There?

Another thing many boys notice when they start puberty is that their testicles (the glands that produce sperm and testosterone) start to get bigger, and the skin on their scrotum (the pouch of skin behind the penis that holds the testicles) gets darker. If this is happening to you, you may also have noticed that the skin on your scrotum is starting to look rougher, too.

You may also discover that because you have more testosterone in your system, you may have more frequent erections. Males are able to have erections (when the penis gets hard and sticks out more) even as babies; this is normal. But when these erections start happening more often (especially for what seems like no reason at all) it can feel pretty embarrassing! Most of the time, if you don't make a big deal out of it, no one will even notice you are having an erection—especially if you are around other kids your age. Chances are, they are too busy feeling self-conscious about their own bodies to notice what is going on with yours!

Morning Surprises

Another thing that can sometimes embarrass boys going through puberty is something doctors call a "nocturnal emission" and everyone else calls a "wet dream." A wet dream is when some semen (the sticky liquid that is stored in the testicles) comes out from a boy's penis while he is asleep. Sometimes when this happens a boy remembers a certain type of dream; other times he just notices a wet spot on his pajamas or on the sheets after he wakes up.

If you don't know about this in advance, a wet dream can seem weird or even a little scary. But wet dreams are a normal part of development, and they will stop happening as you get older.

Some boys get embarrassed when they have a wet dream because the semen can make a mark on the sheets. If you feel this way, you might want to negotiate with the adults in your life to do your own laundry. Then you'll be happy because you will be the only one who knows when you have a wet dream, and the adults in your life will be happy since it means they will have less laundry to do!

Am I Turning into a Werewolf?

Nope, you aren't! A big part of puberty is growing hair in all sorts of places you never had hair before. Often the first place a boy notices hair growing is above his penis. Usually, the next place he becomes a little furry is the underarms, followed by the face, usually on the upper lip. When this happens, the exciting process of learning to shave is right around the corner. Finally, body hair begins to spread over the legs and arms. This can continue even a few years after all the other big changes of puberty have already happened. Some boys develop chest hair long after puberty, even into their 20s, but not all adult men have chest hair.

What's That Smell?: Changes in Your Skin

You may have noticed (or someone might have told you) that you are starting to smell, and not like a flower! As you go through puberty, the sweat and sebaceous (oil) glands in your skin become more active. This makes you sweat more. Because of hormonal changes, your sweat also has a different—sometimes stronger—smell.

Your sebaceous glands are also pumping out more oil, and this is part of what causes acne (also called "pimples" or the slang name "zits") during puberty. Acne and smelliness are normal, but there are ways you can take care of your skin to help decrease problems with both. You can find out more about taking care of your growing body in the next chapter.

Emotional Changes

Have you ever gotten to the point where you are happy one moment, furious the next, and then sad half an hour later? Welcome to one of the hardest parts of puberty: mood swings.

KNOW THE FACTS

Hormones are chemical messengers that help your cells communicate with each other. Everyone has hormones. In boys the hormone that controls puberty is called testosterone; in girls, it's a hormone called estrogen.

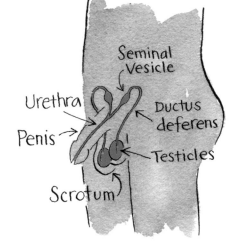

Seminal Vesicle

Urethra

Penis

Ductus deferens

Testicles

Scrotum

The male reproductive system is a pretty amazing bit of plumbing. It consists of the penis, the scrotum, the testicles, and the urethra. As you go through puberty, you'll notice that you grow pubic hair (hair around and above your penis) and that your penis gets larger.

There are at least two reasons for mood swings. The first is the hormonal changes that are going on in your body. Yes, that pesky testosterone strikes again!

The second has to do with your changing place in the world. Puberty is the bridge between being a boy and being a man, and sometimes you might feel like you don't belong either place. You aren't a kid anymore, but sometimes you feel like one inside and still want to do kid things. On the other hand, you aren't ready for the responsibilities that come with being an adult, even though you may feel like you want and need more independence. Some days you might feel out of place and like no one understands what you're going through. No wonder you might be a little (or a lot) cranky!

Talking about your feelings can help keep those emotions in check. Don't worry if it is hard for you to open up—everyone feels this way sometimes. A trusted adult will understand if it is difficult for you to get the words out.

Hey, Am I Getting Breasts?

Actually, boys do have breast tissue under their nipples. About half of all boys develop

The Expert Says

Everyone is concerned about what other people think of them, how their bodies look, and how they compare to others.

23

some swelling under their nipples as a part of middle puberty. The medical name for this is gynecomastia, and it is a normal reaction to hormonal changes in the body. There are no medications that can make this swelling disappear; it just goes away on its own, usually in about six months. If you feel particularly worried about it, talk to your parents or guardians, or a health care provider. Because boys do have breast tissue, all boys have different shaped and sized chests. You don't have to look like someone in a bodybuilders' magazine to be normal!

What's That Cracking Sound: Vocal Changes

When you are between 12 and 14 years old, your voice will start to get deeper. The deepening of your voice happens because of (bet you guessed this by now) the effect of testosterone. This time, the testosterone is working on your larynx (also known as your voice box). The larynx then gets bigger, and your vocal cords get longer and thicker.

For some boys, the voice change happens almost all at once; it seems like they go to bed one night with the voice of a boy and wake up the next morning with the voice of a man. Other guys may have months where their voice is higher at one moment and then lower a moment later. Sometimes a very quick change in pitch comes out as cracking. This might happen at very inconvenient moments: when you ask a question in class or when you are just about to say the punch line of a joke. Fortunately, voice changes seldom take longer than 3 to 4 months to work themselves out. Remember, not all boys end up with deep booming voices! Having a slightly higher voice is normal and natural, too. If someone tries to tell you that you don't have a boy's or man's voice, know that it's your voice and you're a boy, so obviously it's a boy's voice!

A boy's vocal chords grow 60 percent longer during puberty and become thicker. They go from vibrating 200 times a second to 120 times a second.

A QUICK REVIEW OF WHAT'S NORMAL

● First of all, it's normal to feel unsure about the changes in your body. That's why this book was written, to help you sort out some of the questions you might have.

● It's also normal to develop more slowly or quickly than your friends and other boys you know. Every boy has his own pace for physical and emotional development.

● It's normal to feel unsettled about yourself and your relationships. Puberty is a very confusing (and sometimes awkward) time for everyone. Right now, feeling weird is perfectly normal!

● It's normal to have embarrassing things—like your voice cracking during a presentation—happen to you. At the time, it may seem like the worst thing that's ever happened in your life, but in a few weeks or a few months you might forget all about it.

● It's normal to have a body that doesn't look like your favorite social media bodybuilding star, people in magazines, or even other boys you see in the locker room. Bodies come in all shapes and sizes!

● It's normal to want to make changes in your life. You're growing up, and things aren't supposed to stay the same forever.

● Asking your dad, mom, or another adult to help you with whatever challenges you are facing as you move through puberty is not just normal; it's ideal. That what they are there for!

- Growing hair in some unexpected places is totally normal, and if you don't grow hair in some places you might expect to, that's normal too. The hair might start growing in later, or it may not come at all.

- Looking to take on more responsibility and to be more in control of your life (especially if your life seems to be more out of control) is normal. This is the time in your life when you are starting to gain a little bit of real independence, and your behavior will determine just how much independence you can handle at this time in your life.

So don't sweat it. It may take a little while, but sooner or later, you'll find that all these changes have sorted themselves out and you feel perfectly normal!

QUICK TIP

Keeping a journal can help you feel more in control of your emotions. Getting those feelings out of your head and down on paper might help you understand a bit better why you are feeling like you do. You don't have to let anyone read (or even know about) the journal. It can be your secret. You can keep a journal on your computer or get a special notebook to put your thoughts in.

Chapter 2:

THE CARE AND FEEDING OF YOUR CHANGING BODY

It seems like it could be nature's joke that just when boys' sweat glands begin to work overtime, boys often develop what looks like an allergy to bathing. If you are struggling with the adults in your life about taking a bath (which does cut into video-game playing time), remember: now that you are growing up, you have more adult-like sweat glands. This means you are going to have more of an adult-like smell. Even though you may not be able to tell the difference, people around you will. If you get the reputation as the "stinky kid," especially at school, it could be very hard to lose.

Hit the Showers

Showering (or taking a bath) every day (or at least every other day) is your first line of defense when it comes to the "smellies." For best results, wash all your parts (from your head to your feet) with soap. Soap is an important part of this process that boys sometimes forget. If you have noticed that you are particularly smelly, you can get special soap labeled "deodorant," which will help keep you odor-free longer. It's best not to use deodorant soap all over your body, though, because it can really dry out your skin. Just use it on your smelliest parts (usually your armpits and your feet).

You may see advertisements for "body sprays" that can help you smell better (and also climb buildings and learn to skateboard, according to the ads), but often the ones marketed to boys your age are very strong. They are so strong, in fact, that they might make the person sitting next to you gasp or choke. If you really like the smell of these sprays, use a tiny little bit (spray them on for about half a second) and don't use them instead of showering. Body odor plus body spray can cause a not nice smell situation!

Wash Those Hands

Hand washing is another important personal hygiene issue to talk about, and the good thing is that you don't even have to get completely wet to do it! Hand washing is not just about personal hygiene, because germs on your hands (which you use to touch everything) can make you (and people around you) sick. Sometimes it seems to boys that grown-ups are too worried about hand washing, but it is pretty important. If you eat without washing your hands, it's like (yes, this is gross) putting everything that you've

touched since the last time you washed your hands right in your mouth. Not a very nice thought, is it? Yuck!

It's also very important to wash your hands after you use the toilet, after petting or handling any kind of animal, or if you have been around someone who is sick.

You already know how to wash your hands, right? Well, maybe so, but most people don't wash their hands long enough. It really takes 15 to 20 seconds under warm water (with soap) to get them clean. You might want to use a timer (or just count slowly to yourself) to make sure you're washing long enough. Sometimes dirt can get trapped under your nails: there are soft bristled brushes that can help with that. Making sure you trim your nails frequently also makes it easier to keep your hands clean.

Lotion: It's Good for Every Body

You—yes you—can use lotion. Some boys will need lotion after a shower to keep from having dry, flaky, itchy skin, which some people call looking "ashy." You can get lotion made especially for boys, and you can also get lotion that doesn't have any smell added to it at all. If you put it on while you are still damp from the shower, it will be an even smoother process. You might even find that you like how it feels.

Heading Out: Hair

Boys have it pretty easy when it comes to what people expect them to do with their hair. Regular shampooing (which might mean every day if you have oily hair, or maybe even once a week if you have coarse hair) should just about do it.

Some boys use gel to make their hair stay in place. Some gels wash out easily, but some (especially ones that are wax-based) are much harder to get out. If you are going to use a wax-based gel or hair-molding product, you'll have to wash it out every night if you don't want to wake up in the morning with your hair looking like something from a horror movie.

If you have longer or particularly tangle-prone hair, you can buy a conditioner that you can use after you shampoo. If you have longer, coarse hair, you might need a special deep conditioning treatment every week. You can also buy special shampoos for very dry hair to keep you from having dandruff (when skin from your scalp flakes off and makes a mess) and for hair that is

Have you seen how little kids hold their hands over their ears when something making a loud sound goes by? They are smart because they know that loud sounds can hurt their ears. The headphones you wear when you play your music can also hurt your ears if the music is too loud. Chances are, if other people can hear what you're listening to when you are wearing headphones, it is too loud. When you are older, you'll be thankful that you turned down the volume!

exposed to a lot of chlorine (for boys on a swim team).

The Ear from Which You Hear

The most important thing to remember about ears is to not stick anything smaller than your elbow in them. That means no cotton-tipped swabs, no pen caps, and no paper clips! All these items can really hurt your ears if you stick them in too deep. If you are shampooing your hair regularly, that should be enough to keep your ears clean. Still, it doesn't hurt to spend a little extra time scrubbing behind your ears with a washcloth. If you have short hair, the dirt that builds up in that area can be very noticeable!

The wax you have in your ears is helpful: it keeps dirt from getting further down into your ear where it can do real damage. Although it might be tempting to pick at the wax, it's better to leave it alone and let it do its job. If your ears feel clogged or you have trouble hearing, talk with your health care provider, an adult you trust, or your school nurse about things you can do to help get rid of some of the wax.

Oh, Eye See

What are those two things in between your ears? Oh, wait, they're your eyes! I'm sure we don't need to tell you how important your eyes are to you; you're probably using them right now to read this book! The main thing to remember with your eyes is that if you are having trouble seeing, you need to tell the adults in your life so you can get your eyes checked. Some people have trouble seeing things that are close to them. These people are far sighted. Most people who have trouble seeing, though, are near sighted, meaning they can see things that are close to them, but have trouble seeing the blackboard (or smartboard) and other things that are further away.

If you do have trouble seeing, you might need glasses. Lots of people have glasses, and they come in all kinds of fun colors and styles. While they might be difficult to deal with at first, you'll get used to them, and you might even forget you have them on! If you're worried about liking your first pair of glasses, ask your friend to go with you when you go to pick out your frames. They might give you the confidence to feel like you're picking something awesome and stylish. After you've had glasses for a while, you might look into getting contact lenses. Some boys feel more comfortable about their appearance while wearing contacts, while others find it easier to play sports wearing contacts rather than glasses. Contacts do take a certain amount of care, so talk to your parents (and then an eye doctor) to find out if they are a good option for you.

Putting Your Best Face Forward

The easiest way to take care of the skin on your face is to keep it clean. You can wash your face when you wash your hands, but try to use a gentle, non-perfumed soap. Don't use deodorant soap, since it will leave a light film of deodorant on your face, and no one (no matter how smelly) needs deodorant on their face. You should also make sure to put on sunscreen before heading outside, since sun exposure (and sunburn) can irritate your skin and cause other problems.

Another very common problem that boys have with the skin on their face is acne. Who gets acne? Almost everyone! Nine out of ten preteens and teenagers have to deal with it. It might seem like some kind of mysterious plague, but there are some things you can do to tame the "zit monster." Acne is caused when excess oil gets trapped in your pores, combines with bacteria (i.e., germs) and dead skin cells, and develops into what we call a pimple. Washing your face can help reduce acne, but don't do it too often. If you wash your face more than three times a day or too harshly (you can't scrub your face like you scrub a dirty pan), you will just irritate your acne, not make it better.

Even though it is very tempting, don't pick or pop your pimples! It can irritate your skin and cause an infection, and can even leave a permanent scar. You can buy creams at the drugstore to help with acne. Follow the directions and don't use more than the label says; benzoyl peroxide and salicylic acid (the most common ingredients in over-the-counter acne creams) can be very irritating if you use too much. If you feel like your acne is out of control, talk with the adults in your life about going to a dermatologist (a doctor who specializes in skin and skin problems).

Remember, despite how obvious your zit might feel to you, a lot of the time other people are too busy worrying about their own zits to think much of yours. After you finish puberty, you'll likely find that most (but not all) of your zit problems disappear. Just hang in there until then!

Keeping Your Awesome Smile Looking Awesome

As you get older, the adults in your life will start expecting you to take more responsibility for yourself, including your oral hygiene (which is a fancy way of saying mouth care). Even though there is no longer an adult standing over you making sure you brush your teeth, now is the time to build good habits that will keep your teeth looking good for the rest of your life.

You probably know someone (maybe a grandparent) who has lost their teeth and now has fake ones that they take out at night and keep in a cup by the bed! We know a lot more about dental care now than we did when they were young, so losing your teeth to tooth decay does not have to be a usual part of getting older.

Brushing is the most important thing you can do to keep your pearly whites, uh, pearly white.

● Look for a toothbrush that has soft bristles, since a toothbrush that has hard bristles can actually make tiny abrasions in your gums and lead to more problems! Replace your toothbrush every three to four months, since the bristles tend to wear out by then and can't really get your teeth clean. Plus, bacteria can start to grow on your toothbrush after a while, so you'll just be sticking germs back into your mouth!

● Don't forget to brush all the surfaces of your teeth: outside (the sides touching your cheeks), inside, and all the flat surfaces. Make sure to brush your teeth in small circles to help keep them squeaky clean. You should brush your tongue, too, because bacteria can hide there and lead to very smelly breath!

● Remember, in order to get your teeth really clean, you need to brush them for two to three minutes, which is a longer time than you might think. Using the timer on a microwave or your cell phone can be a good way to find out if you're brushing long enough, or pick a song that is three minutes long and play that while you brush. Don't sing along though—you might bite yourself!

● Besides brushing, flossing is another important thing you can do to help your teeth and gums stay healthy. Flossing removes food bits and bacteria from between your teeth, and it helps prevent cavities and keeps your gums strong.

Do I Have to Go?: Boys and the Dentist

Although you can do a lot to help your teeth and mouth stay healthy at home, you also need a check-up and cleaning at the dentist's office every six months. Not all families have health insurance, and not all health insurance plans cover going to the dentist, but there are still ways to get dental care. Your school nurse can probably give you some ideas of how the adults in your life can make that happen.

Some people (not just kids) don't like going to the dentist. If this is the case for you, make sure you ask questions before you get to the dentist's office. Ask the adult who made the appointment for you why you have the appointment: Are you only having your teeth cleaned or do you need something more done? Then, when you get to the dentist's office, before you open your mouth and say "ahhh," ask the dental hygienist or the dentist to explain exactly what is going to happen, step by step. Some procedures at the dentist's office might be uncomfortable, and the more information you have about when and how things might not feel so good, the more you can prepare yourself. A surprise birthday party might be a fun thing, but a surprise in the dentist's chair is anything but fun!

Tiny Little Train Tracks: The Drama of Braces

Lots of kids (and adults even) have braces. But even though braces are very common, sometimes even hearing that they might have to get braces makes boys sweat.

The most common reasons people need braces are because their teeth are crooked or because their upper and lower jaws are not the same size. Both of these problems can make it harder to care for your teeth. Braces don't just improve your smile; they can make your entire mouth healthier.

Getting braces is a perfect time to start taking more responsibility for your health. Ask your orthodontist (a dentist that specializes in braces) about how you should care for your braces, what kind of foods you should avoid, and what you should do if part of your braces breaks off, gets bent, or irritates the inside of your mouth.

Shaving

The first place you will probably have hair on your face is on your upper lip and chin. It will probably be just a little teeny amount (like the fuzz on a peach). Some boys and men remove this by shaving. Some boys who have a coarser hair texture don't shave and instead use a special depilatory powder made for men and boys who get "bumps" when they shave.

There is no medical reason to remove the hair from your face, but many boys find they are more comfortable without it. If you do decide to shave, you might only need to do it every few days when you start out because the hair won't grow that quickly. The best way to learn about shaving is to talk to a male adult in your life (or an older brother) and get him to show you how to do it. For many boys, their first shave feels like an important part of becoming an adult.

Arming Your Underarms!

Another possible weapon in your personal fight against "the smellies" is deodorant. Not everyone (including grown-ups) wears or needs deodorant, but if you want to try it, look for the type that says only "deodorant" and not "deodorant/antiperspirant." Antiperspirant contains chemicals which actually block your sweat glands, which is not as healthy for your body. Some deodorants have a stronger smell than others, so you might have to try a few different kinds to find what smells best on you and works best with your body chemistry.

YOUR FIRST SHAVE

When you are ready for your first shave, it's best to get your dad, big brother, or another adult to walk you through it step-by-step, but here are some tips that will help the whole process go, um, smoother.

● First, choose a razor. There are two types of razors: electric and manual. An electric razor needs to be plugged in, or at least charged, while the manual (or disposable) types use old-fashioned arm movements. Manual razorblades are disposable, so when the blade wears out, you usually just throw it away and get a new one. A lot of people think that electric razors do not shave as close as the manual razors.

● If you choose a manual razor, you will also need some type of shaving cream or gel to apply to your face before shaving. These creams and gels help lubricate your face and help reduce the risk of nicking or cutting your skin.

● The best time to shave is after taking a warm bath or shower to make sure your skin is hydrated and soft.

Now it's time to shave:

Step #1: Lather up! Apply the shaving cream or gel to the areas you are going to shave.

Step #2: Make sure to go with the grain of your hair, not against it. Shaving against the grain (or upward) can cause rashes or red bumps.

Step #3: Don't rush and don't push down too hard with the razor. If you do, you're likely to cut your face. It's better to go over a part of the skin twice—lightly—than to press down hard. Ouch!

Step #4: After shaving, wash your face with soap and water.

Step #5: Follow up your shave with a face lotion or moisturizing aftershave product. This will help prevent your skin from drying out. If you're heading outside, be sure to apply sunscreen with a sun protection factor (SPF) of at least 15 (higher if you have fair skin).

Congratulations on surviving your first shave. You'll soon be an expert since it is something many men do every day.

Tip: Ask your mom or dad to get you an antiseptic styptic pencil. To use: dip the white pencil in water, and then apply it to any nicks or cuts to stop bleeding immediately.

Tip: Change razors or blades frequently. A dull blade can irritate your skin and cause rashes. You are also more likely to cut your face with a dull blade.

Some deodorants
can leave marks
on your clothing.
The marks are
particularly
noticeable on
dark-colored
clothes and when
you are wearing
tank tops. To cut
down on these
marks, look for
deodorants that
say they dry
"invisible."

Meet Your Feet

Although you might not think about your feet as body parts that need much care, they do some of the hardest work for you. It's worth taking a look at what they might need to function best and what you can do to help them out.

First of all, feet need good, supportive shoes that fit properly. Especially as you are growing quickly in these fun-filled (ha ha) puberty years, you should be measured with the foot-measuring thing (it's called a Brannock Device, but that makes it sound kind of scary) every time you buy shoes. Did you know it's important to measure both feet? Your feet can grow at different rates, and having a too small shoe can make you pretty sore after a while!

Feet can be some of the smelliest parts of the body. This is because nearly everyone's feet sweat a lot. And since bacteria that can contribute to smelliness grow best in places that are not only damp, but also dark, you can see why taking off your shoes can sometimes be a frightening experience!

Foot care is really no different than caring for any other part of your body, except that you have to wash your feet with a little more energy if you really want to get them clean. Make sure you separate each toe, because bacteria can get stuck in there and contribute to general smelliness. Make sure you dry your feet carefully afterwards and change your socks every day.

One common foot problem is called "athlete's foot," which is not always caused by being an athlete. Athlete's foot is a fungus, and it can turn your feet into an itchy, smelly mess. If you have itchy feet and what looks like extra dry skin on the bottom of one or both of your feet (especially where your toes meet the ball of your foot), you might have athlete's foot. When you first get it, it can usually be treated with a special kind of medicine called an antifungal that the adult who is responsible for you can buy at almost any drugstore. It's important to treat athlete's foot right away because it can spread to even less fun parts of your body. Maybe you've heard of "jock itch?" Ewwww. If the antifungal doesn't get rid of your athlete's foot, or if it spreads to the area on or near your toenails, you may need medicine you can only get from a health care provider to heal it up.

Get Dressed

Showering every day helps stave off the smellies, but you also need to change your clothes as regularly as you can to keep smelling good. Unfortunately, you can't tell by looking at it if a piece of clothing is clean or dirty. For example, a T-shirt that you wore to school all day might not have an obvious spot or stain on it, but if you sniff the underarms?

Pee-ooo! That's why it's best to keep your dirty clothes and your clean clothes far away from each other. That way you will be able to know the difference without doing the "sniff" test, which might not tell you for sure anyway.

Am I Normal?

Many boys find all the changes coming their way confusing. You might be worried that if you don't change at the same time— or in the same way—as other kids, that you might get teased or feel like a freak. It's true that it's not easy to be seen as different from the other kids around you, but there really isn't much you can do about it. Your body will develop when it's ready.

One thing that will help is to have a parent or other trusted adult to talk these things over with. There are also books like this one, as well as websites where you can find helpful information about your changing body and your changing life. You can even check out the resources section in the back of this book for some books and websites that might be helpful.

Remember, you're the expert on your own body, and if something doesn't seem right or feels weird or painful, tell an adult you trust. The more you can learn about your body and the way it works, the better your lifelong relationship with your body will be!

It's also really important to remember that boys come in all shapes and sizes, and this is normal and natural. You might not have big muscles like some boys you know, and maybe you're rounder than some boys, but bodies don't look all the same, and there is no wrong way to have a body!

Eating Healthy for Growing Boys

You might be really tired of hearing this, but eating right—and we don't mean potato chips for breakfast, cookies for lunch, and candy for dinner—is really important at this time in your life. Your body is working hard to grow and it really needs healthy food to do what it needs to do. Try to eat three healthy meals a day, starting with a nutritious breakfast. Eating fruits and vegetables at every meal will also help you keep at a weight that is good for you and will give you the energy you need to do all the fun things you want to do (and the boring stuff you need to do).

Every time you turn on the television, you're likely to see an advertisement for some new diet pill, diet system, or contraption that will help people lose weight or keep them from getting fat. The reason there are so many of these systems, pills, and contraptions is because very few of them work in the long term. If you are concerned about your body size or weight, the answer is definitely not fad diets, pills, or starving yourself.

Instead, what you need is to get good nutrition and the right number of calories to keep growing and keep going. Dieting makes food the enemy, and food isn't your enemy; food is fuel and it should be fun! Learning to make good choices when it comes to your food can be part of the fun of growing up.

Make sure to work with your body, not against it, to keep healthy. Your body sends signals to say, "I'm hungry," and you should be sure to listen. It's important to know what hunger feels like for you. When you are eating because you're hungry instead of just because you're upset or bored, it's easier to make healthier food choices.

Also, try to make food choices based on how you feel after you eat certain foods. For example, when you eat potato chips, do you feel good afterwards? Do you feel like you have a lot of energy? Is it easier or harder to concentrate in school if you've had oatmeal for breakfast instead of a donut? Do you find the "zit monster" attacks after you've eaten oily foods? Does eating a banana before practice keep you from feeling hungry all the way through practice? What if you eat a chocolate bar?

FAST FOOD TIPS

Fast food is easy, cheap, tasty, and let's face it, it's everywhere. Since fast food isn't going to disappear anytime soon, you will need to take charge and make your own healthier choices as you get older. Again, don't think about "good" and "bad" foods. There are no specific foods that are good or bad, but some foods don't really fuel your body very well. Many fast food choices are in this category.

● Sometimes a salad can be a good fast food choice, but beware of adding lots of dressing or other random bits of non-vegetable type food. Those don't add much nutrition, but can add a lot of calories. It's like putting a fully loaded hamburger on your salad!

● Fast food is highly processed; in other words, it's been a long time since it looked like the food that someone grew, if it ever was. Plus, because it comes from so far away and has been frozen, canned, or bagged, it takes a lot of preservatives and chemicals to make it taste good. These preservatives and chemicals make it harder for your body to use fast food as fuel.

● When in doubt and there is a fruit option, consider taking the fruit.

● Just because the drink that comes with a fast food meal has the word "juice" in it, that doesn't mean it's healthy. Watch out for sweeteners like high fructose corn syrup, which your body has a very hard time using for fuel.

● Think about training your taste buds. It's true that French fries taste great, and fast food French fries taste especially awesome because they're often sprayed with a sugar solution before they're fried, but apples can taste pretty great if you get in the habit of eating them.

● Make small changes first. If you usually eat an entire fast food meal and drink a large soda, maybe you can start with carrying your own water bottle and eliminating the soda. After you've done that for a while, maybe switch it up from French fries to apples.

HEALTHY EATING ON THE MOVE

Here are some foods that are easy to grab when you are heading out the door and need a snack:

- A granola bar
- Nuts
- An apple
- A navel orange
- Baby carrots
- A banana
- Pretzels
- Grapes
- Crackers

- A cheese stick
- Yogurt
- Cereal
- Graham crackers
- Peanut butter on celery
- Toast
- A mini whole wheat bagel with cream cheese

Sports: One Way to Work Your Muscles

As a little kid, you naturally moved around a lot. If you have a little brother or sister, you might get tired just looking at them running around. However, as we get older, we spend more time in school and doing homework and less time moving our bodies. Sometimes, the only time school-age kids get to jump and run around is a very short recess!

Team sports are one way to work your muscles, keep your body active, and have fun, but they definitely aren't the only way. Sometimes, boys feel pressured to be good at sports. Sometimes this pressure comes from family members, parents, coaches, or

The Expert Says

Sometimes parents behave worse than the kids when it comes to sports. Try not to let it get to you if the adults around you are taking the game too seriously.

friends. Sports might seem like the only way to be popular at your school. While playing a sport well is great, your goal should be to enjoy yourself. Only a few boys will grow up to be professional athletes, but every boy can enjoy being a part of a team.

Some reasons to play a team sport are to:

● Have fun.

● Get exercise and enjoy what your body can do.

● Learn skills like how to pass and dribble, as well as self-confidence, self-discipline, and teamwork.

● Make friends.

● Release stress and pent-up energy from sitting still all day.

Notice that "win every game" wasn't listed as a reason to play. Yes, winning is fun, especially compared to losing, but if there is too much emphasis placed on winning, sports actually become less fun. If the only thing that makes sports fun is winning, and only one team can win, that means only half the players get to enjoy it! Would you and a bunch of your friends go to a movie you knew half of you would hate? That would be a waste of time. Sports are the same way if the only goal is winning.

If losing is particularly hard for you, you can set personal goals for each game that don't depend on winning. For example, if you're an outfielder, your goal could be to catch 80 percent of the fly balls that come to you. If you struggle to support your team mates, maybe your goal could be to find five things to compliment other players about.

Sometimes adults push kids too hard in sports. While pushing yourself a little can be good, pushing yourself and your growing body too much can lead to permanent injuries. If you are feeling so much pressure that sports have lost some of their fun for you, it might be time to talk to your parents or the other adults in your life about this.

Sports Safety

Sports accidents do happen, but there are lots of things you can do to prevent serious injury. One of the most important things you can do is to wear the right protective gear. Your head is super important since it's where your brain is kept. It's also one of the easiest parts of your body to protect by simply wearing the helmet made for the sport you're playing. Have your coach adjust the helmet for you and always use the chin strap (if the helmet comes with

QUICK TIP

Wear a pair of baggy boxers over your protective equipment and no one will know you are wearing it.

one). Otherwise, your helmet might go flying one way and your head flying the other way at the exact moment when they should be sticking together! You also need to wear a helmet when you're riding your bike. In some places it is even the law that you need to wear your helmet, and the adults who are in charge of you can get into trouble if you ride without one.

For some sports, like soccer and football, you might also need to wear protective pads. Wear them even if they're uncomfortable; otherwise, you will be much more uncomfortable later.

It is also very, very important to protect your genital area. There are two pieces of equipment that can help protect your penis and testicles: a cup and an athletic supporter (also known as a jockstrap). A cup is a hard piece of triangular plastic that, despite its name, looks nothing like a drinking cup. It goes inside your jockstrap and protects your genitals from direct blows, either from another player (for example, during a tackle or a tag play at home) or from equipment (the ball, a flying bat, etc.). Most kids call the whole thing together a cup. When you are in a hurry it might feel like wearing a cup and jockstrap is too much bother, but if you've ever been hit by a ground ball that takes a funny hop, you know that even with a cup it can be very painful. Without a cup, you risk permanent damage. If other boys in the locker room give you a hard time about wearing a jockstrap or a cup, tell them to mind their own business or do the final adjustments in the bathroom stall so that the protection of your private parts is kept private.

Another very important way you can keep from being injured when you play sports is to warm up and stretch out before you start. Warming up and stretching give your muscles a chance to wake up and get the blood flowing so you can perform at your best without getting hurt. There are special areas of your body you'll need to concentrate on stretching for different sports. Your coach should know all about this. If you are playing a sport that doesn't require teams or coaches (running or skateboarding, for example), you'll have to do your own research about stretching out. Someone more experienced in the sport may have some ideas, or you can check your sport's related websites for more info.

The final word of advice for staying safe when playing sports: don't play if you are hurt. It's easy to get caught up in the excitement of the final play or a close game, but playing when you are hurt can turn a small, not-so-serious injury into one that can give you problems for a long time. Since you're going to need your body for the rest of your life, it's not worth doing permanent damage! Anyone who asks you to play when you are actually injured is not respecting you or your body. You won't just be doing yourself a favor by taking yourself out of the game, you'll be helping your entire team be the best they can be.

Keep It Moving: Beyond Team Sports

Little kids naturally move around a lot. However, once kids go to school and have to start sitting still more than six hours a day, they slow down. Often the only time kids get time to jump and run around is at a very short recess. Then, to make it worse, as kids get older, organized sports become a more and more important part of outside play and physical education. Sometimes kids who aren't Joe or Janet Jock stop enjoying moving their bodies and become more sedentary. This is not healthy, and it's definitely not fun. Team sports are definitely not the only way you can move your body and maintain your health.

Even if you're not a basketball superstar, there are lots of ways you can make physical activity a part of your life. You can:

● Try individual sports, or sports that don't require a whole team to participate, like running or tennis.

● Experiment with activities that you might enjoy but that aren't competitive. Yoga is a good example. No one loses at yoga!

● Go for walks. There's a whole world out there to explore, even without leaving your neighborhood.

● Go for hikes (hikes are basically walks where there are lots of trees).

● Relearn active games you might remember from when you were younger, like tag or kickball. You might want to stay away from dodgeball, which too often causes hurt feelings or worse!

● Suggest social activities with your friends that involve physical activity. Maybe go for a bike ride together or go in-line skating.

● You could always play the kind of video games that require you to run in place, jump around, or dance.

● Explore ways to get around that involve movement, like running, walking, or riding a skateboard or scooter (with protective equipment, of course).

● Go swimming on a hot day. If you haven't been moving in a while, swimming is an especially good choice because it's easy on your joints!

● Go to the mall. Yes, that's right, the mall. Walking around the mall can be good exercise. Some malls even open early to give walkers a safe place to get moving.

You can probably come up with even more fun ways to get your body moving if you think about it. Remember, people come in all different weights, heights, sizes, and shapes. If you can develop loving habits that take care of your body now while you're still young, you will be healthier—and much happier—as you grow up.

Performance Enhancements: Don't Risk It

It's natural to want to develop bigger muscles or be the best at your sport, but all kinds of surprising things can happen to your body when you use steroids. Your testicles can shrink, you can grow breasts, you can lose your hair, get depressed, stop growing, or even die. Some of the effects of steroids are reversible; some are not. Remember that a good body and better physical fitness is something you have to earn through practice and training, not through drugs. Don't risk your future just to have bulging biceps now!

Yawn: Boys and Sleep

When you were younger, your parents were more likely to enforce a strict bedtime. Now that you are older, you may still have a bedtime, but getting enough sleep is starting to become more and more your responsibility.

The average boy your age needs 10 hours of sleep a night in order to grow and be healthy, but you might need a little bit more or less than that. If you have trouble waking up in the morning, can't concentrate at school, or fall asleep during class, it might not be because you're bored—you just might not be getting enough sleep.

What if you have trouble getting to sleep? One of the things you can do to help yourself is to create a bedtime routine. If you do the same things every night, it will help your body recognize, "Hey, it's time for sleeping now!" A bedtime routine might look something like this: get in your pajamas, brush your teeth, say good night to your parents, read for 15 minutes, and then turn out the lights on another great day.

Another thing you can do to fall asleep quicker and sleep better is to put away the screens! Looking at the kind of light that comes from tablets or smartphones actually tells your brain to be awake. It can be pretty fun to huddle under the covers texting your best friends until late at night, but when those late nights turn into cranky mornings, it might not be worth it.

Wetting the Bed

Some boys (more than you might think) have trouble with wetting the bed, even into their teen years. It is so common, in fact, that this problem has a special name: nocturnal (nighttime) enuresis. This is most

QUICK TIP

If you tend to wake up in the middle of the night remembering things like, "Oh, I can't believe I didn't tell Mrs. Walker I can't mow her lawn next week," keep a pen and paper by your bed so you can jot these things down.

59

MORE TIPS FOR SLEEPING WELL

DO stay away from caffeine in the hours before you go to bed. You probably already know that certain types of soda contain caffeine, but did you know that chocolate does, too?

DO avoid stimulating activities. For some boys, this might mean not watching action or horror movies, reading exciting books, or playing "just until I reach the next level" of a video game—at least, not right before bed. All these things are fun, but they aren't really relaxing.

DO avoid arguments or other things that might upset you emotionally right before you go to bed.

DO pack your bag and lay out your clothes for the next day. If you think you might forget something (like materials you need for a special project) write yourself a reminder note.

DO avoid screen time in general right before bed. It makes it hard for your brain to transition into the most restful type of sleep.

often caused by being a very deep sleeper, but other things can contribute to it as well, including a delay in the way your brain and bladder communicate with each other, a lower amount of a hormone that controls how much urine you make, or a smaller "functional" bladder, which means that while your bladder may be a normal size, when you sleep it sends a signal that it is full earlier than it needs to.

In some cases, nocturnal enuresis runs in families, so if you wet the bed, there is a good chance that someone you see at the family reunion did, too. If you are wetting the bed, talk to an adult in your life about it. There are many simple things that can help with bed-wetting, but it's best to get checked out by a doctor before you start any program of your own. This will help make mornings (and sleepovers) a much more pleasant experience!

The Expert Says

In the U.S., between 5 and 7 million children 6 years old and older suffer from primary nocturnal enuresis, or nighttime bed-wetting.

Chapter 3:

FRIENDS AND FEELINGS

This is often the age when people start telling boys, "You're getting to be a man now; you have to stop all the tears."

Even if "those people" are your grandparents or someone you love, they really don't know what they're talking about. You don't need to stop all the tears. In fact, it's really important to cry when you need to. Crying is a way to release strong feelings, and if you don't ever have that release, it can cause problems for your mental and physical health.

It's unfortunate that there are some people who will make you feel worse if you cry in front of them or make it harder for you by teasing you. If you are around a lot of people like that, it can help to make a deal with a really good friend. Agree that part of your friendship is being each other's "safe space," and that you will never tease each other about crying.

I'm Driving Myself Crazy: Dealing with Out of Control Feelings

While it's important not to keep your feelings bottled up, you (and your parents) might be frustrated by how moody you've become since you started puberty. You may feel cranky and ready to run away from home one minute, and want to hug everyone and do a little happy dance the next. No matter how much your teachers, your parents, and even this book reminds you "this is normal," it's still no fun.

If you find yourself having trouble managing your feelings, you might want to ask your parents or guardians to help you come up with coping strategies to deal with stress. Sometimes even using very simple tools can help you feel a lot better.

For example, sometimes it can be helpful to keep a stress log, which is basically a mini calendar where you write down what's bothering you when you feel especially worried. This can help you find patterns of what causes you to worry or stress. Here's an example: if you're always stressed out on Thursday nights and you don't know why, keeping a stress log might help you realize it's because you have pop quizzes on Friday in math, your hardest subject. If you know that, you can use that information to figure out a way to lessen your stress trigger. In this case, you might decide to get extra help in math so it doesn't seem so hard and make you so stressed out. You could also approach this situation in another way: you could do all the rest of your homework for the week before Thursday night so that you would be a little calmer on Friday since you have less to do. The key is to figure out what is causing your personal worries and try to make them a little easier on yourself.

Addressing the things in your life that are making you feel out of control is one part of emotional management (which is fancy talk for figuring out how to live with your feelings) but you still may have a lot extra emotional energy bouncing around inside. Here are some things you can do to help level out some of your moods:

● Try not to get overtired or too hungry. Hunger and tiredness can cause crankiness all by themselves, and adding them to your hormonal mix makes things much worse! If you feel like you are starting to lose control of your emotions, get yourself a healthy (non-sugary) snack and a big glass of water. Sometimes just sitting down for a minute to eat and drink is enough to let your emotions settle back to normal.

● Remember that feelings are not good or bad, they just are. Yes, it's more fun to feel happy than to feel sad, but it isn't wrong to feel sad. In fact, feelings give you information about yourself and your world. For example, if you always feel irritated or angry after you spend time with a certain friend, maybe there is something happening that you need to talk with that friend about.

● Writing in a journal can help you deal with strong emotions. Writing about what is going on with your feelings can not only help release some of the extra emotional energy, but also can help you figure things out. If you are worried about someone reading what you've written, find a good hiding spot for your journal and get one with a lock on it. It may not be the best idea to take it to school with you, because if you lose your backpack, you could lose your privacy along with it.

● Sometimes physical activity helps get out all your stored up emotional energy when nothing else can. That might even be why schools started having recess! You can shoot hoops, ride your bike, or even just go for a long walk. If you're at home and can't get away and do anything else, sometimes just yelling into a pillow will work wonders!

● Talking can help, too. If you just want to let off steam, your best friend might be able to help you. If you need some guidance or advice, a trusted adult who respects your boundaries is also a good choice. If you are having particularly strong feelings, a trained professional (such as your school counselor or a psychologist) should be able to help you sort out your feelings and give you some suggestions for making your emotional life easier.

● If nothing else works, get involved in a fun activity that will get your mind off of your strong feelings. You can play a musical instrument, listen to your favorite CD, read, or complete an art project.

Another very powerful way to keep stress from getting the best of you is to always be thinking about a bigger goal or something you are working for in the long term. For example, let's say you're a boy who cares a lot about animals and you have the goal of helping five puppies from a local shelter get adopted. If you went out to start putting up signs to tell people about the puppies and it suddenly started raining, you might be annoyed about the rain, but you probably wouldn't be as stressed out about it as you would be if you weren't so concerned about the puppies. The bigger goal helps you not be as stressed about the little things you can't control.

Making Friends

As if it isn't enough that your body and your feelings are changing, many boys find this is an age where they have to make a whole new group of friends!

Sometimes this happens because you are going to a bigger middle school and the kids you used to hang out with are in different classes and have a different schedule than you. Sometimes the crowd that you hung out with when you were younger starts doing things you don't like, and you need to find a new crowd to hang out with. Sometimes you just find that your interests have changed and you don't have anything in common with your old friends anymore.

Whatever the reason, making new friends can be scary but ultimately rewarding.

If you are having trouble finding and keeping good friends, you might try making a list of the qualities that you are looking for in a friend (for example, sense of humor, likes to do the same things, even-tempered). Look around to see who has those qualities—it might even be someone you weren't expecting!

Some friendships just happen, but more often you need to make a special effort to find good friends. Being friendly (waving to people, smiling, cracking jokes with them) is a good beginning. Be interested in your new potential friend. Ask them questions about their likes and dislikes, how things are going for them, or what kinds of things they like to do after school.

One way of really cementing a friendship is by doing things together besides watching TV. Activities that don't require you to interact much can't help you get to know your friend very well. Try going to the park, playing a board game, or building something together instead.

If you want to change crowds, you can sometimes start by making a few new friends. Eat lunch with someone new, or chat with them between classes. You can find things you have in common this way.

QUICK TIP

Don't assume that someone doesn't want to be friends just because they don't say hi to you. The person could be really shy and afraid to make the first move.

Friendship Skills

Although in some ways it's natural to be a good friend to someone you care about, there are skills that can make being a good friend easier.

For example, everyone makes mistakes in friendships: we say something that we don't mean when we are tired or angry, or we let our good-natured teasing go too far. One of the surest ways to keep a friendship growing strong is to apologize when you do something to hurt your friend's feelings. It works best if you don't say, "I'm sorry but…" and then go on to explain to the person why they are wrong. That's not really an apology; it's a way of keeping an argument going!

Another thing that helps keep a friendship growing is talking through disagreements before they get really big. If a friend borrows your baseball glove and doesn't bring it back when he promised to, it's better to mention it the first time he does it and not wait until the 10th time and blow up. He might not even know that it bothers you until you tell him.

Another important building block of friendship is being a good listener about big and small things. When your friend has a problem, most of the time they won't need you to give them advice and won't need you to come up with a solution. They probably just need you to really sit still and listen to what they have to say. Sometimes this isn't easy. Your friend might want to talk about a movie that you thought was stupid. Interrupting with "booooorrring" might make your friend laugh the first time, but it won't feel great when they do it back to you. If you make the extra effort to pay attention to what your friend has to say, you might become more interested in the conversation and decide the movie wasn't stupid after all!

When friends are going through hard times, you can help by offering to assist them with tasks that might be overwhelming for them. You might have to help them figure out what you could do that would be helpful. For example, if your friend breaks his arm and has to spend a few days in the hospital, you could offer something like, "I could help you by going and picking up your homework at school, or I could bring you some magazines to read. Does one of those sound like something that would make this day better?"

Just as your friends should expect you to be there for them during stressful times, you can expect the same things from your friends. If you need help, call them. If they need help, be there. Together you will make it through all the challenging times that growing up can dish out.

A FEW MORE TIPS ABOUT BODY LANGUAGE AND LISTENING

When you're talking

with anyone (a friend or a teacher or a parent or another adult), it's important to show that you are listening and that you are not just waiting for your turn to talk. It can be helpful to wait a few moments after the other person stops speaking before you start. This can be really hard sometimes if you are excited about the conversation or nervous.

Another great way to move the conversation along is to ask questions. This might come naturally when trying to understand the story, but you can also say things like, "Really, wow, what happened next?" or, "So what did you say then?" or, "And what did the next text say?"

Try to avoid bored-sounding responses like, "Uh huh" or, "Mmmmm," which make it seem like you are thinking about something else, even if you aren't! Part of being a good listener is learning to read body language. You probably already do this a lot of the time! If a friend has balled-up hands and a very red face but says, "I'm OK," you might notice that their words and actions aren't matching up and should ask them another question or try to comfort them.

Your body language matters too! If you are squirming or looking away or messing around on your phone while your friend, teacher, or family member is talking, it looks like you are not interested in what they have to say. Crossing your arms in front of you can make it look like you are not open to what they are talking about, or even that you are mad!

Instead, lean toward the person a tiny bit while they're talking and make eye contact as they speak. You don't want to actually stare at the person— that can seem creepy. Just look into their eyes naturally so they know you are listening.

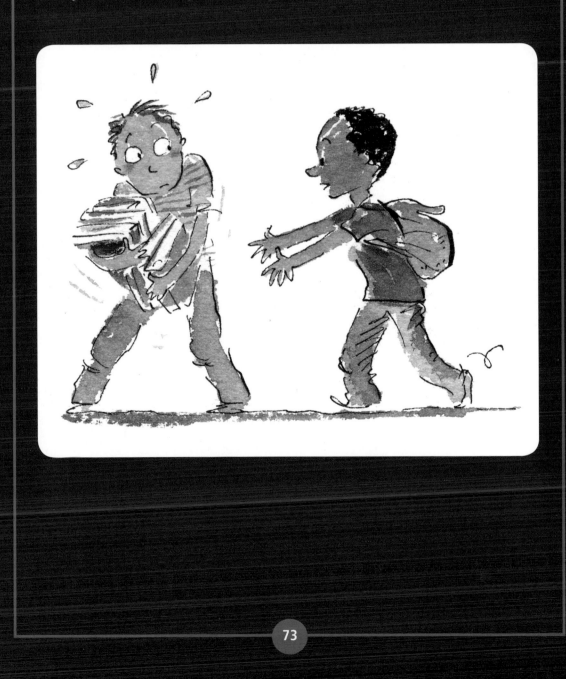

Is a Crush a Must?

Sometimes people pressure boys in puberty to start looking at girls a little differently or suggesting that the way they interact with girls must change. At this point in your life you may have started to crush on girls, or you might be completed uninterested in any kind of romance.

This is a time in your life when you are exploring relationships and getting to know yourself better. Don't put pressure on yourself to start the dating part of your life too soon. If you are interested in dating or "going out with" someone, work on being friends first. Try different fun activities where you can get to know that person. Going to the movies (a very typical first date) doesn't allow for much talking, so it might not be the best way to get to know someone. In fact, there will be less pressure for both of you if you go out with a few other friends (they can be on a date or not) for a group activity instead of hanging out one-on-one.

If you feel a lot of pressure from your friends to jump into dating before you are ready, it can help to make at least a few friends who are running at your same speed when it comes to romantic relationships.

The good news is whether you feel interested or ready for dating or not, all the friendship skills you are building in these years will help you when you are ready.

Personal Empowerment

A boy's life can feel like a roller coaster when he's smack-dab in the middle of puberty. One minute you might feel super happy, but the next moment you might feel extra sad. Add this to all the changes your body is going through and the fact that you're trying to figure out how to build middle-school-type friendships, and it's a lot of difficulties to handle all at once.

A healthy (or even growing) dose of personal empowerment during these years can help your days be smoother, even if they aren't always easy. Personal empowerment is a pretty simple concept; it just means having a feeling or sense of your own power.

If you have a sense of your own power, you will still have the same problems. You'll have pimples you can't control, your friends may turn out not to be friends, and sometimes your basketball team will lose.

But when you have a sense of your own power:

● You understand that you have control over some things in your life.

● You are able to make changes when there are changes to be made, so that you can jump over obstacles or maybe kick them over.

● When you can't change a situation, you find ways of dealing with the reality that you have to live with and don't blame yourself or other people for life not always being perfect.

The adults in your life have hopefully been working with you since you were an infant to develop a sense of personal empowerment. Here are some things you can do to develop this valuable life force of your own:

● Read books (fiction is good, but nonfiction is even better) about boys like you who overcame difficulties and then went on to accomplish great things. Pay close attention to what kind of help they had, how they used the resources they had access to, and what they did when they got discouraged.

● Keep your friends who like all of you (your personality and who you are in the world) very close to you, and make sure they know how much you appreciate having them around!

● Spend less time with friends who put you down. There's one of these in every crowd: a guy (or girl or adult) who always has to be the star and who complicates everyone's lives by always knowing how everyone should be acting at every single moment and then getting mad when the world doesn't cooperate with them. This person can often be charming and fun when you first start being friends, but then you will start to notice anytime you have a disagreement they always talk you into taking the blame!

● Learn how to ask for help. As one principal used to say, "Closed mouths don't get fed." No boy can do everything by himself, and what's the fun of that anyway?

● Find activities that stretch you just enough. Sometimes it's easier to be a boy who only takes the classes he knows he can get an A in, or who only plays the one sport he has been playing his whole life. But if you don't reach for something just a bit more difficult, you won't grow.

● Ask the adults in your life for help figuring out how the hard things in your life can help challenge you or help you grow in a positive way. There is a saying; "Whatever doesn't kill you makes you stronger," and that does seem like a bit of an exaggeration. Some hard stuff that doesn't really cause you any physical harm (like parents getting divorced) might just make you more tired and sad, not really stronger. But some challenges in your life can inspire you to dig deeper and find more enthusiasm or energy.

CONSENT AND BOUNDARIES

As more of your life takes place when your parents or guardians aren't watching, you have to develop your own ethics and boundaries.

One area you need to be really clear about is only touching people when they want to be touched. Your body belongs to you and people should not touch it without your OK, also called your consent. In the same way, other people's bodies (including kids of all ages) are theirs, and you shouldn't touch them without their consent.

This includes touching that you think is a joke. For example, especially when a girl first starts to wear a bra, a boy might think it's funny to snap her bra strap through her shirt. This isn't fun for girls (it actually hurts) and it's not funny because you are touching someone without their consent.

It's really important to respect physical boundaries, but it's just as important to respect other people's privacy, which is another form of boundaries. Don't look through someone else's phone or things if they haven't given you permission, or push them to talk about things or answer questions they don't want to answer.

You can think of another person's body, personal space, belongings, and private thoughts like their own little house they carry around all the time. Just like you wouldn't barge into someone's house without knocking and asking to be let in, you should ask and then wait for permission before you go inside their boundary house.

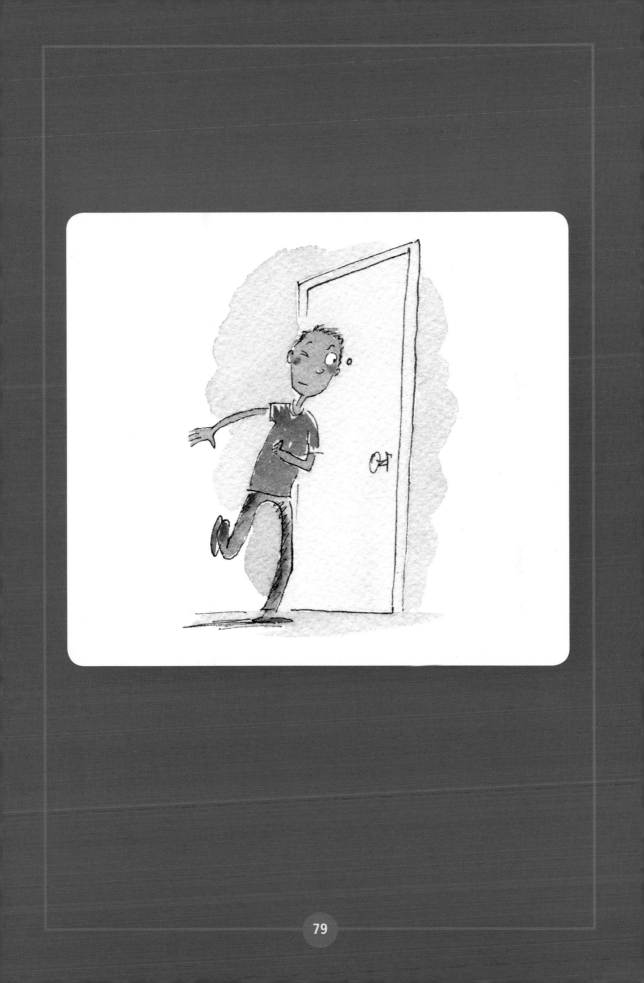

Chapter 4:

WHAT DO THESE PEOPLE WANT FROM ME?: CHANGES AT HOME

You might have noticed this book sometimes talks about the "adults in your life," "adults at home," or "guardians," as well as using the more specific term "parents." That's because not all boys are raised by their parents. Some boys are raised by a single parent, grandparents, two moms, two dads, in foster families, blended families, by aunts and uncles, or combinations of the above. We want those boys to understand that this book is for them, too. Every family is unique and different from every other family. What's important is that you have an adult in your life whom you can trust.

The process of going from being a kid to being an adult is mostly about taking more and more responsibility for more and more bits of your life. This goes on until you are managing

most of your everyday choices yourself, or until you become, as the saying goes, "the boss of you." The truth is you're never totally the boss of you. We live in a complex society. Even when you are an adult there will be some people (like your boss at work) who will have the power to enforce consequences if you don't follow the rules. Of course, your boss probably won't give you a bedtime, tell you what kind of TV shows you can watch, or insist you eat your vegetables before you have dessert (but you never know).

Responsibility and You

Most of the common everyday conflicts that happen between boys in the transition between childhood and adulthood and the adults in their lives center around issues of responsibility. The adult may not think a boy is responsible enough, for example, to make choices about seeing a certain movie or going to a certain party. The boy thinks he definitely is. Sound familiar? Of course, the opposite can be true as well. The adult may think a boy is old enough to mow the lawn and take out the trash; the boy thinks that's too much responsibility for someone his age.

Some conflict between teens and preteens and the adults in their lives is normal, even healthy. The job of kids as they get older is to separate from the adults in their life until they are independent enough to live on their own. The job of these adults is to give kids loving guidance, set limits, and make sure they are actually ready to live on their own when the time comes.

You've probably noticed that you don't have control over what your parents or guardians do, but you do have control over what you do. One big step you can take toward getting to do more things that you want to do is to work on building your parents' trust in you. The easiest way to do this is to do what you say you are going to do when you say you're going to do it. If you agree to help your little brother with his homework after school, take the time to help, even if you'd really rather watch something (anything even) on TV. If your parents or guardians give you a time to be home, make sure you're there on time, even if everyone else has a later curfew and is bugging you to stay just a "few more minutes." If you say you are going to a party, be at that party, not somewhere else, unless you call and get permission first.

Curfews and Other Rules

Curfews are often a hot-button issue for adults and kids. This is a perfect time for you to work on the art of the compromise. Sometimes your parents or guardians will let you come in later if they know you are safe when you are out. Work with them on what you would do if, for example, you

QUICK TIP

Offer to call or text message your parents or guardians to check in when you are out with friends. Always have a plan for getting out of unsafe situations.

got to a party and there wasn't an adult there, or kids were drinking. If your parents know you have a way to stay safe, they'll feel better about being flexible with your curfew.

If you and your parents are constantly fighting about rules in the house, ask for more details about their expectations. For example, a common rule adults make is: "Kids must keep their rooms clean." Well, to you, "clean" might mean no fungus growing on the carpet, while to your parents or guardians, "clean" might mean that your bed is made every day and that you vacuum twice a week.

Chores

Most families have expectations about how kids help out. This might include small things like clearing the table after dinner, or bigger things like housecleaning, or even helping with a family farm or store. These expectations can be a source of conflict between boys and the adults in their lives, especially if boys feel like helping around the house cuts into their social time too much.

Luckily, there are some ways to negotiate about chores so that everyone will feel like they are getting some of their needs met.

If you and your parents or guardians are feeling frustrated around the subject of chores, ask for a family meeting to discuss things. Prepare for the meeting beforehand by thinking about what areas need to change and what compromises seem reasonable to you. It might help to come armed with some additional areas of chores that you might be willing to do to help the house run smoothly in exchange for having fewer responsibilities in another area. For example, if helping with dinner puts too much pressure on you to get home quickly after sports practice, maybe you could ask what you could help with in the morning instead.

If the adults in your life complain that you are not doing a good job at the chores you are doing, ask for more details about exactly what they expect to be done. Try making an actual list by breaking the chore down to its smallest parts and checking each of them off as you do them.

BOYS SAY:

I GET AN ALLOWANCE FROM MY PARENTS BASED ON THE NUMBER OF CHORES I ACCOMPLISH EACH WEEK. IF I WANT TO HAVE MORE MONEY, I HAVE TO DO MORE CHORES. THAT SEEMS FAIR TO BOTH ME AND MY PARENTS.

-Dwayne, age 13

Oh Brother (or Sister): The Art of Being Friends With Siblings

Siblings can be absolutely infuriating! You may get angry if they take something that is yours, go into your room without asking, or bother you when you have friends over.

Your older brothers or sisters may try to boss you around and tell you what to do, and your younger brothers or sisters may borrow your things or want to be around you all the time when you just need a break and want to be left alone.

Brothers and sisters can be really fun, but that doesn't mean it's easy for siblings to get along.

Some things that might help:

● It is common for younger kids to feel like their older siblings get to "have all the fun" and do whatever they want. Older brothers and sisters often think that the baby of the family gets more than their fair share of attention. Try and remember that there are good things and bad things about whenever you came into your family, and most times these things even out in the end.

● Don't be confused if you feel both proud and jealous of your siblings, sometimes at the exact same time. If you are feeling jealous of what your siblings have done, remind yourself that you have special skills and talents that they don't have.

● Did you know you can make "just between siblings" rules? For example, if you and your brother run into problems when you tease each other, you could agree never to tease each other where nonfamily members can hear, or you can agree never to tease each other about certain things.

● Older brothers and sisters can really help make this time in your life easier if you ask them. If you're the oldest, remember to be there for your younger siblings when they get to be your age.

You might not believe it now, but your brothers and sisters may be the best friends you have throughout your life. If you invest in your relationship with them now, it will really pay off later on.

THE CARE AND FEEDING OF PARENTS:

HOW TO TALK SO THEY WILL LISTEN

What else can you do to help your relationship with the adults in your life go better? Lots of things. For example:

● If you end up in a mess, let them know as soon as you realize it and ask for help. You are going to make mistakes sometimes, and most parents remember this. Covering up your mess almost always guarantees a bigger disaster in the end.

● Tell them how you're feeling. It may seem like they can read your mind, but they can't.

● Adults are people too, so make sure to talk to them like they are! Try talking about something you both are interested in or asking about when they were a kid.

● Try not to roll your eyes at them. Eye-rolling often drives even the calmest people wild.

● If you are in the middle of a discussion that is turning into an argument, ask to take a break and calm down.

● Listen to your parents or guardians and ask questions. Show that you are trying, at least, to understand their point of view.

● Pick your battles. You don't care about everything equally, so try to give in without a big discussion on some things you care less about. The adults in your life will listen more closely when you bring up an issue if they don't feel like you are always complaining about every rule they make.

Chapter 5:

YOUR CHANGING BODY IN THE OUTSIDE WORLD AND AT SCHOOL

Do you remember your first day of kindergarten? You might have been worried about not being able to get to the bathroom in time, missing home a lot, or not having much success with scissors. Now that you've successfully dealt with all those challenges, it might be just the tiniest bit frustrating to find that each year in school brings with it new and improved things to worry about!

As you get older, parents, guardians, and teachers (and therefore, kids) talk a lot more about grades. Some schools give marks like "satisfactory" or "needs improvement" in earlier years, but by third grade, many schools have switched to the more common A, B, C (well, you know the rest) system. This makes a lot of kids nervous because they seem more like "real" grades that will count and cause them trouble in the future if they don't do well. Depending on where you live, you might also have to take what are called high-stakes tests, or tests you need to pass to progress to the next level or graduate from junior or senior high school.

Sometimes boys put lots of pressure on other boys to not do well in school because they don't think it's "cool" to get good grades. If this is happening to you, talk with an adult you trust about it. This can be a hard situation to handle, especially if the kids who are teasing you about your good grades are old friends. You've probably heard the term "peer pressure" (pressure other kids put on you to be, act, or dress like them), and this is a perfect example. One thing an adult can do is help you figure out ways to meet other kids who like to study and don't mind being thought of as "smart." Also, ask your teacher for help in keeping your grades private. Teachers sometimes like to praise their best students in front of the other kids, but they might not know about the trouble it is causing you!

It's true that school life for boys in the older elementary grades or middle school can be difficult in some ways, but exciting things are happening, too. You probably have a little bit more freedom, like being able to choose a few of your classes or even teachers. You might have more fun classes that give you opportunities to do things like learn to play an instrument. Plus, you might have new chances to hang out with other students, learn things together, develop some of your talents, and even find some new talents you didn't even know you had!

Studying: Yes, It's a Skill

There isn't room in this book for all the information we could include about study skills. If you are interested in learning more about how to study, your school librarian can point you to entire books on the subject. However, there are a few simple things you can do right now to make your study time more effective:

● The very first thing you need to know about homework is what your homework is. Keep a small notebook with all your assignments in it and you'll never be left wondering what is due when. Unless you lose the notebook, that is, so try not to lose that notebook!

● Set aside a special time to study every day. For some kids, right after they get home from school works best. Other kids need a break and prefer to dig into their books after they get something to eat and have some time to relax or do other chores.

● Find a quiet place to study. If home doesn't work, try your school or community library.

● Don't wait until the night before a project is due to start it; if you have any questions or don't understand something, you won't have time to get the answers you need!

● Having trouble concentrating while you're doing your homework? Set a timer on your phone or the clock on the microwave to help you work your "sticking to it" muscles. If you hate math, promise yourself that if you do nothing but your math homework for 30 minutes, you can take a break or move on to something more fun.

● Unless you really must use the computer for the assignment, choose a spot far away from the internet. Watching one more YouTube video of someone who taught their dog how to water ski is always going to seem more interesting than algebra. You can also use site-blocking software so you won't be tempted to check social media "just for a minute."

93

QUICK TIP

This is the time to start keeping a little notebook (or a big, huge notebook if you need it) where you write down all your assignments and check them off when they're done. You'll be able to have more fun hanging out after school if you can look at your notebook and see you've got everything taken care of! You can also use your assignment notebook to remind you of the things you need to take to school in the morning.

A QUIZ:
WHAT DO YOU KNOW ABOUT GRADES?

If you get a good grade, it means you've learned a lot. If you get a bad grade, you haven't learned anything. True or false?

Answer: False! Grades are one way of showing how much you've learned, but they aren't perfect. Sometimes a lower grade in a hard subject means you actually learned more than a higher grade in a subject that's easy for you.

Even smart kids can sometimes get bad grades or have a hard time in school. True or false?

Answer: True! The grades that you see on your report card do NOT mean "dumb" or "smart." There are lots of kinds of intelligence. Even if school is not that easy for you, you can bet that you have special skills somewhere else, even if you haven't discovered them yet.

If you are getting a bad grade in a subject, just give up, quit school, and move to Australia, there's nothing you can do to change it. True or false?

Answer: False! Just because you are getting low grades in a subject, it doesn't mean you aren't good at that subject, or that your grade in that subject has to stay low. Talk to your teacher about what you need to do to bring the grade up.

You should like all subjects equally. If you don't like math and spelling the same amount, there is something very, very wrong with you. True or false?

Answer: False! It's normal to have some subjects that you like and some subjects that you don't. After all, haven't grown-ups been asking you, "What's your favorite subject?" since kindergarten? In fact, if you do the homework for the classes you like least first, you can use the homework for the classes you like more as a reward for yourself!

If you are having trouble in school, you can get help from:
a. Your teacher after school
b. Summer camp
c. After-school study groups
d. Your neighborhood library
e. An adult at home
f. The guy who feeds the lions at the zoo

Yes, you guessed it, every one but "F." And you could ask the guy at the zoo, but please don't distract him while he's feeding the lions. If he ends up being cat food, he won't be much help to you.

I don't think much of a man who is not wiser today than he was yesterday.
—ABRAHAM LINCOLN

Getting the Help You Need: Learning Disabilities

Some boys learn better by reading information from a book, some boys learn better by doing an experiment, and other boys might find it easier to understand information that they hear in a song or a podcast.

While all boys learn in their own unique way, some boys experience specific challenges in learning called learning disabilities. A learning disability makes it more challenging for the brain to work with information. Having a learning disability doesn't mean you're not smart—it just means you might need special types of assistance to learn. You might need medication to help with some of the symptoms of your learning disability, extra time to take tests, or a specially trained teacher who can help you figure out the best strategies for you.

Certain learning disabilities can also impact the way you talk and play with other kids because you might have trouble understanding what their social cues mean. For example, some boys might not be able to tell when other kids are joking and when they are being serious.

There are many ways schools and families can support boys with learning disabilities. Every child with a learning disability should have something called an Individual Education Program (IEP), which describes the kind of support and help he gets at school. An IEP is when all the people involved in helping the boy learn sit down together and figure out the best plan. If you are diagnosed with a learning disability, you can contribute to the writing of your IEP. You will need to talk to the adults about how learning is hard for you and what makes it easier. It might not be easy if you are just getting comfortable with the idea of having a learning disability, but learning to advocate for yourself (that is, how to fight for what you need) is a valuable skill for any boy to develop!

If you have a learning disability that makes some types of schoolwork hard for you, it's important to remember all the other things you do well. A boy who might take a long time to finish a math test might read more quickly than everyone in his grade, while a guy who has trouble chatting casually with his classmates might be able to complete projects quickly or learn chemistry with what seems like no effort at all!

Sometimes adults or other kids will be curious about the special classes you have. Just because someone asks you a question doesn't mean you have to answer it. Aside from people who need to know (your teachers) or people you might want to know (like a supportive friend or two) you don't have to tell anyone how your brain works. If you'd like to explain your learning disability to people who can advocate for you, ask one of your IEP teachers to help you write a short explanation. You don't have to share it, but at least you will have it handy.

Getting Along with Teachers

If you ever want to get a grown-up talking, ask them to tell you about their favorite teacher. Then, ask them about their least favorite teacher. Never ask these questions if you have somewhere to be soon—those questions usually lead to very long stories!

The fact that grown-ups will talk so fondly (or not so fondly) about things that happened so long ago might remind you how important teachers are to all kids. Hopefully, you've already had a few teachers that you really liked. You've probably also had some teachers that you didn't like as much. This is very normal.

Although you might not have a lot (or any) choice about who your teachers are right now, you do have choices about what to do when you have a difficult teacher/student situation.

If a teacher is getting on your nerves, it might be tempting to think, "You're not the boss of me!" Except for, well, when you are at school, they are the boss of you. If you are having trouble getting along with a teacher, try and think of it as a chance to learn a very important grown-up skill. Just like a boy might have to learn from a teacher he might not like, grown-ups sometimes have to work for bosses they don't get along with. It might not be easy for you, but there are some things you can try to help your school life go more smoothly.

While it's normal to have some teachers you like and some you don't, if your relationship with your teacher is making it hard for you to learn, there are some things you can do to improve the situation. One thing you can do if you are having trouble getting along with a teacher is to try and give it a little time. Especially at the beginning of the year, teachers have a lot to do, like setting up their classrooms and getting books and supplies ready. You might find they act differently when things settle down further into the school year. Since every boy and every teacher is different, it might take time for you and the teacher to figure each other out.

Since you can only change your own behavior, it's best to look at that first. Do you show up on time? Do you do your homework? Are you respectful? Do you ask questions when you don't understand something? If you answered no to any of these questions, try changing your own behavior first. If your teacher has some "pet peeves" (behaviors that particularly annoy or bother them), getting along might be as simple as not doing those things!

If things don't seem to be getting better, talk to an adult you trust. This can be a parent, family friend, etc. While talking to someone your own age is good for letting off steam, other kids might not have the experience to help you completely sort out the problem.

If none of this helps, ask an adult if they would help you set up a meeting with the teacher. Sometimes just talking about the problem directly—especially if you have an adult who understands you and can help you explain yourself if you get stuck—can really help a lot.

As you go through school, you will have some teachers who you feel really close to and some that you can't wait to say goodbye to at the end of the year. If you can figure out how to learn from all different types of teachers, you will gain some very important life skills that will help you a lot in later years.

It's Not Just About the Books: Extracurricular Activities and You

For now, school is your primary job, and because some boys struggle more than others with schoolwork, some days it might feel like you're

NON-SPORTS ACTIVITIES

Don't like sports? No problem! Try:

- Writing for the school paper.
- Taking pictures for the yearbook.
- Playing chess on the school chess team or in the school chess club.
- Singing in the choir.
- Acting in (or making sets or designing costumes for) the school play.
- Running for student government.
- Helping plan dances or other fun events (many schools have a social committee for things like this).
- Learning about running and fixing electronic equipment in the AV club.
- Learning about another culture and language in (for example) a Spanish club.
- Performing a stand-up comedy routine in the school talent show.
- Playing a musical instrument.
- Volunteering as a tutor to someone who needs help.
- Working behind-the-scenes for a sports team keeping score or helping the coach.

failing at your job. Those days it's nice to have some extracurricular activities to let off some steam, learn new things, and remember life is more than just geometry and science. Most schools, especially as you get older, have many different kinds of opportunities for having fun, making friends, and learning what you are good at.

If your school doesn't offer an activity you'd like, you can always suggest it. If you can't find any groups or clubs you like at your school, often community centers, youth centers, and religious organizations have activities for boys as well.

Here are some tips to make your extracurricular activities extra special:

● Don't take things too seriously. Involvement in outside organized activities can be a really great way to develop self-discipline and learn how to do your best, even when you don't feel like it. However, if you are too intensely focused on achievement and winning instead of just having fun, you miss a lot of the experience. There are plenty of places where life puts pressure on you—don't add to it!

● Honor your schoolwork. Teachers say that after-school jobs can contribute to kids getting lower grades and being super tired in school. If you really want to work as you get older, it's best for your schoolwork to pick jobs where you can decide when to work (like mowing lawns) or to work very limited hours, like on the weekends or only one or two evenings a week.

● Mix it up. Involve yourself in some activities that are physically active, and some that require more brainpower than muscle power. This is the time to be trying lots of different activities, so you can find out what you like.

● Use extracurricular activities to explore career choices, but don't be in a rush to decide. If you think you want to be a doctor or a nurse, it might be great for you to volunteer at your local hospital when you get old enough. The real-life experience might be enough to tell you, "Wow, this is exactly what I love," or, "Man, I really can't stand the smell of hospitals one bit!" At the same time, just because you couldn't handle hospital smells at 13 doesn't mean you won't be fine with them by the time you go to college. You have plenty of time to grow and explore!

● When looking for activities to try, think outside the popularity box. You don't have to be good at sports and cheerleading to make good friends. Try joining the school newspaper, taking pictures for the yearbook, running for student government, or even playing chess on the chess team.

● Build some "downtime" in your life. Just hanging out with your friends is an important part of growing up. Everyone—adolescents especially—needs time to be relaxed without the pressure of some structured activity.

Dress for Success

When you were little, your mom probably picked out your clothes for you. Now that you're older, it can be fun to express yourself with your clothes and to see how far you can take your personal style and experiment with different fashions and see what looks best on you. There are a lot of different types of fashion out there and that means every boy should be able to find a style that suits him.

Keep in mind, if you opt for jeans with a ton of rips in them or try that style where the jeans are so big that they actually fit you somewhere around your ankles, you are sending a message to those around you. Similarly, wearing a suit and tie on a daily basis also sends a message. The trick is to match your clothes with the message you want to send.

We're not saying that it's fair that other people judge you based on your clothing choices and personal appearance, but unfortunately people do. You might think your style says, "I'm too cool to care that I'm wearing a stained thermal shirt," but some folks might think it shows that you're lazy or careless, even if you're not.

When you get dressed in the morning, ask yourself, "What do my clothes say about me?" If you think people might be getting the wrong message, change the channel by changing your style.

"WHAT DO MY CLOTHES SAY ABOUT ME?"

Chapter 6:

STAYING SAFE IRL AND BEYOND

Throughout this book, we've mentioned that every boy has social changes that go along with the physical changes of puberty. This is the time when boys become more involved with their friends and less involved with their parents and family. It might feel strange to be less connected with a parent or grandparent, but as you get older, you will most likely find ways to have relationships with them that reflect the adult you are becoming instead of the kid you used to be.

Interactions with Adults

You might not feel as close to the adults at home as you once did, and that's normal, but try not to shut them out emotionally. Maybe your mom won't be the first person you talk to about a smaller problem at school, but you can still share some of your day with her. These daily interactions will be the building blocks for when you need more serious support, and for your future adult friendship.

Even though you are separating from your adult primary caretakers, this doesn't mean that you need adults in your life any less. In fact, it's more important than ever to have solid, dependable adults around who can support you.

How do you find adults who are not only safe for you to spend time with but who can also support you in a way that will help you grow and push you to be your best? Most of these folks will come in your life in a natural way: a teacher, a relative, a coach, or someone who works at your house of faith (church, synagogue, or mosque). You might also connect with the parent of a friend, an aunt or a grandparent, or with a mentor who is high school or college-aged. There are also youth mentoring programs in many areas that connect well-screened adults with kids who want mentoring, specific kinds of support, or who are interested in a particular career. If this sounds like something you'd like, ask your guidance counselor at school about programs that might be available in your local area.

When you're building a friendship with an adult, there might be different rules about communication than there would be with your friends. Many adults don't like to be connected with the young people they work with on social media, or your teachers might only accept friend requests from former—not current—students. This is just to protect your privacy and the privacy of the adult; it's almost never anything personal. Also, adults may or may not want to text with you about plans and to exchange information. Depending (to some extent) on the adult's age and (to a much greater extent) their familiarity with technology, you might not be able to use the latest emojis or text abbreviations. And make sure you use the title you would in person (e.g., Mrs. or Dr.) when you text or email.

When building relationships with the adults in your life, you will need to be thoughtful about your own personal safety. This is a very, very, very important point to remember: it's not the position of the adult (teacher, priest) or their relationship to you (aunt, parent of a friend) that makes them safe for you to spend time with; kids are sometimes hurt by the very people that should be protecting them. What makes an adult safe is that they always respect your boundaries.

Adults who help you at school or in extracurricular activities or are in your family shouldn't ask you to keep secrets about your friendship with them, and your friendship with an adult should feel different than one you have with people your own age.

Hopefully you have been told many many times by now that your body is your own, and no one has the right to touch you in a way that makes you feel confused, sad, uncomfortable, or scares you. No one, except for sometimes a doctor in a doctor's office, should touch you anywhere in your private areas (the areas usually covered by a bathing suit). Even if that person is someone your family knows, a relative, or someone who is very nice to you or pays special attention to you, they still don't have the right to touch you in these areas. If someone does try to touch you in a way that doesn't feel right to you, it's not your fault. It's never your fault when an adult doesn't respect your private areas, even if they say it is. If this happens to you, you need to tell your parents or another adult you trust as soon as possible.

Peer Pressure

The biggest thing to remember about peer pressure is that whatever they say everyone is doing, everyone is not doing it. Resisting peer pressure can be hard—some boys say it is one of the most difficult things about these in-between years. Here are some tricks you can use when dealing with other kids who want you to do something you don't want to do:

● Practice saying "no" when it isn't super important. This will help you be thought of as someone who doesn't just go along with the crowd. Often kids will stop pressuring you if they know you aren't going to give in, because it makes them look silly.

● Physically remove yourself from situations in which you feel pressure to do something you don't want to do. If you know that the boys in the corner at recess are going to be plotting their next wedgie victim and you don't want to be part of the mean wedgie-giving gang, don't walk by them and take the long way around.

● Ask a good friend or a trusted adult to help you brainstorm ways to deal with things kids say when they are trying to get you to do something you don't want to do. You can even make up flash cards to carry around with you to remind you what to say.

● Have a "peer pressure" buddy. If your friend sees you struggling to say "no" to something everyone else seems to be saying "yes" to, they can jump in with, "Well, I'm not going to do it either." Having one person on your side feels totally different than going

it alone. Just make sure you return the favor for your friend!

● You don't have to give a detailed answer for every decision you make. Sometimes just saying, "No thanks," and nothing more can be a powerful way of communicating that the conversation is over. Remember: "no" is a complete sentence.

● If you are having trouble saying "no," remind yourself what you are saying "yes" to. For example, saying no to a cigarette is saying yes to fresh breath and healthy lungs.

● Finally, remember even adults have to deal with peer pressure, so learning how to manage it now might be hard, but it will pay off big in the future.

The biggest thing that can help you deal with peer pressure is feeling confident in yourself and in your abilities. As you get involved and find things you are good at, you will feel able to resist the pressure because you know more about who you are and what you want in life.

Bullying and Teasing: How to Protect Yourself

Bullying and peer pressure are two different things, although sometimes they can feel pretty much the same. Basically, bullying is peer pressure amped up to the highest degree. If another kid says you won't be cool if you don't smoke a cigarette with them, that's peer pressure. If another kid threatens to beat you up if you don't smoke a cigarette, that's bullying.

Bullying can be more than physical threats. Someone can bully you by saying a lot of really mean things about you over time, or they can threaten to tell a secret that will cause you problems if it gets out. Even writing mean words on your locker is a form of bullying. If you are getting bullied, it might feel hopeless, but there are things you can do to protect yourself.

First of all, remember that getting bullied is never your fault. You have to really believe this. It's in the best interest of the bullies to make you ashamed of who you are, or whatever they want to bully you about.

Tell your parents, teachers, or a trusted adult right away if you are being bullied. If that adult won't do something, tell another adult. Keep telling adults until you get some help.

Wherever most of the bullying is happening, try to spend less time alone in those physical spaces. If you're getting bullied at school, ask a friend to walk to class with you each day. If you're getting bullied in your neighborhood, walk home with a bunch of kids instead of by yourself. If you are getting bullied on the bus, sit right up front near the bus driver or near a patrol, instead of toward the back.

Find support for whatever it is that the bullies are teasing or bullying you about. For example, if you are getting teased for getting good grades, make sure you hang out with other brainy kids.

There is often safety in numbers, and as an added bonus you can see how they handle any negative attention they might get.

Bullies often get away with their behavior because no one is willing to step forward and say, "Stop!" Studies have shown that if even one kid stands up for a kid who is being bullied, the bullying often stops or become much less frequent.

You can be that kid who steps forward and says, "Stop!" Yes, it takes bravery. Yes, it could mean you draw some negative attention to yourself, but it can also mean that someone's life gets so much better just because of you, and that's one of the best feelings in the world.

Also, someday, you might be looking for someone to step up and say, "Stop!" when some bully is bothering you. That's much more likely to happen if you've done the same for someone else.

Being Brave Without Becoming a Bully

The middle school years are hard for many boys because you are in between everything. You're not quite an adult, but you are definitely not a kid anymore. You're not doing the kind of interesting activities that

BOYS SAY:

TRY TO BE FRIENDLY TO EVERYONE, WHETHER THEY ARE POPULAR OR NOT. THAT WAY, YOU ALWAYS KNOW SOMEONE WHEN YOU GET TO A CLASS OR WALK DOWN THE HALL. YOU ARE NEVER ALONE.

-Andrew, age 15

high schoolers get involved in, but you're not just learning the basics in elementary school either. You haven't become a full adolescent who spends a lot of time straining against parents' rules and pressure, but you aren't attached to your parents the same way you were even a year or two ago.

The unstable self-esteem that comes from all this in-between business is part of what fuels the dramatic increase in bullying and peer pressure in the junior high years. It's hard to be bullied in school, but it's just important that you don't become a bully yourself. Most kids who are bullies have been victims of bullying in the past and taking up the mean-and-tormenting baton is how they try to make themselves feel better.

Anytime you are crossing someone's boundaries (whether that person is a boy or a girl) you are acting like a bully. For example, just like you have the right to decide who touches your body, everyone else has this same right. You don't have to be hitting or punching someone in order for the touch to be unwanted; kissing, holding someone down, or tickling them when they don't want to be tickled are all examples of this.

You have to be especially careful of this when the amount of power you have is bigger than the amount of power the other person has. For example, it can be harder to say "no" or "stop it" to someone bigger or older, or someone who has more friends standing around.

If other students at school seem to be scared of you, go out of their way to avoid you, or if you have a sense that you get more fear than respect from other kids in your class, it's possible that you've fallen into patterns of acting like a bully. Ask a trusted adult if there is someone you can talk to who can help you with this behavior and can support you having healthy friendships.

Sometimes you can end up behaving like a bully just because you're hanging out with kids that like to torment and tease other kids. Once you watch someone do mean stuff to other students, it starts to become easier to do these same things yourself. Ask a teacher or another adult you trust to help you design an escape plan from the not-so-awesome friend group.

Personal Safety: Maintaining Those Boundaries

It's not fun to listen to grown-ups talk on and on about how dangerous everything is. Let's be real, boys, not everything in the world is dangerous, and certainly not everyone in the world is out to do something bad to kids. However, in order to feel safe and secure, you need to develop certain skills to help you recognize safe and unsafe behavior, and you need to have good boundaries between yourself and the rest of the world.

Another thing that both adults and other kids might do that crosses boundaries is access private information without permission. For example, if your friend picks up your phone and reads your text messages, that is crossing a boundary because they are not respecting your right to privacy. You can tell friends that this behavior is not OK with you, and you can also help the people in your life feel safe by not snooping around in their personal emails, texts, or social media messages. If you are worried that there is something that your friend is doing or saying behind your back, finding out about it by reading their private messages won't help the friendship. If you talk with them about your worries, even if what they say hurts your feelings, you'll understand much more clearly and will be able to move forward.

There are things you can do out in the world that will help maintain your boundaries. For example, of course you shouldn't talk with strangers, or get into a car with someone you don't know well, or accept gifts from adults you don't know. You should also make sure not to give any personal information about yourself to people who don't need that information. This includes information you may give out electronically, for example by filling out entry forms for contests or posting personal information online.

If you are home alone after school or while your parents are at work, it's best not to broadcast this fact. Always ask to see the badge or identification card of anyone like a police officer or a gas repair person who comes to the door—you can even check the badge through the peephole; that's what it is made for! Always check with your parents to see if they are expecting anyone before you open the door. When in doubt, don't open the door; just tell whoever it is to come back again some other time.

Building a Great Reputation and Staying Safe

Whenever you hear a grown-up say, "Mmmm, that person has gotten themselves a reputation," you know they probably don't mean anything good. But just like you can get a reputation with other kids at school, you can also build a good reputation with everyday actions. Even though you can't control what anyone else says about you, you can take steps to build and protect a good reputation. Why should you care about your reputation? A good reputation is important because it helps people trust you. A boy with a good reputation has an advantage because adults and his friends expect him to be responsible and helpful, instead of expecting him to behave in a negative or a destructive way. Building a good reputation is all about showing people around you that you have good character. There are lots of things that go into good character, but some of the most important are:

● Being truthful with your friends, family members, and other adults. This is even more important when you have to be honest about doing something that is going to have negative consequences.

● Acting responsibly, especially by doing what you have agreed to do, even when it's hard.

● Having self-control to do boring things when you'd rather do something else will pay off in the long run (like homework).

● Not becoming involved in drama for its own sake. While it's true that what adults call drama boys sometimes think of as "figuring stuff out with your friends," if you want to decrease the drama in your life, the quickest way is to decrease how much you talk about people behind their backs. It can be a hard habit to break at first, but it will make your life much simpler.

Staying Safe in Electronic and Virtual Worlds

The internet can be a pretty amazing place. You can communicate with friends and far-away family members, learn more about your favorite hobbies and interests, play games, learn random trivia tidbits to impress your friends, and watch a lot of videos of cats doing cute things.

The number one thing you need to always remember and never forget is that nothing you post or share in the cyber world (or through any kind of electronic connection) is ever really private.

Before you send that text or photo out there, ask yourself, "Would I be OK with everyone in the whole world knowing what I am saying right now or seeing this picture? Not just the person I am sending this to, but everyone? My family, my teachers, my principal, every single one of my friends, my babysitter when I was 4, and even total strangers?"

Even things you post on supposedly anonymous apps or videos that "disappear" after they are watched don't always stay private. Anything can be screenshot or screen-capped, and once it's out there, it's out there forever. You lose control completely; anyone can share it and anyone can pass it around. You've made a digital trail that can continue to follow you long after you've hit send.

The trail doesn't have to be made on purpose to cause you problems; the person you share a photo with can be a best friend who would never ever betray you or share the photo without your permission. But what happens if they lose their phone at school and the photo gets into someone else's hands? Even if it's just a goofy photo of you waking up in the morning with hair sticking straight up, you might not want everyone in the world to see it.

Also remember: almost everyone you meet online is a stranger. And the trustworthy adults in your life have warned you about talking to strangers, right? If someone you don't know in real life contacts you online and wants to meet with you, tell a trusted adult. Online, anyone can say they are a kid, or even use someone else's photos to make a fake profile.

If you're playing games online that involve other random players, be especially careful that your screen-name doesn't give away any information, and make sure you know how to report abusive messages or cyberbullying in the game environment.

Also, think carefully before sharing personal information such as locations (for example, "checking in" on different social media sites) or the fact that you're home alone (e.g., "Watching scary movie while fam is out, jumping at every noise LOL") to everyone with a phone or a computer.

It's also important to respect your friends' and family members' boundaries on social media. Talk with your friends about whether it is OK to tag them in photos and check them into locations, and be careful about what you post on their wall or write in response to their posts or shares.

Finally, use hard-to-guess passcodes and change your passcodes frequently. One easy way to make a memorable passcode is use an entire sentence, complete with punctuation, or even switch out some of the letters for numbers. "Il0vemyd0gFid0." is going to be much easier for you to remember (and harder for others to stumble into or figure out) than a string of random numbers or your birthday.

Don't ever use your birthday or your name as your passcode.

Cyberbullying

Cyberbullying is any kind of bullying that takes place using electronic technology like cell phones, tablets, computers, or any other device you can use to get online. Cyberbullying is not that different from everyday, in-person bullying, but at times it can be even more harmful because:

● Cyberbullying can happen anytime, anyplace. You don't have to be anywhere near the person bullying you to feel scared or threatened.

● In the electronic world, things can be spread far and wide in no time at all.

● Cyberbullying can make school bullying worse by continuing it 24 hours a day, 7 days a week.

● People who engage in cyberbullying don't have to see the face of the person they are hurting; this means their bullying behavior can get out of control even faster.

● Online, it's easy to post anonymous information or hide behind a fake profile so bullies don't have to take responsibility for their actions.

So, what can you do about cyberbullying? Like bullying in real life, being the victim of cyberbullies is never your fault. But you can do certain things to protect yourself and the people you care about:

● Say something. If someone is threatening you, spreading rumors about you, sharing your private information, forwarding your messages, or engaging in cyberbullying, immediately screen-cap the bullying content (if possible) and then report them to the application or software for "terms of service" violations. In most apps targeted to kids your age, the report function should be very obvious. If it's possible, block the screen-name and then tell a trusted adult right away. Information and gossip spreads fast on the internet, so acting quickly is important.

● Protect personal information. This means choosing effective passcodes and logging out of your accounts when on a shared computer. It also means not letting yourself be pressured into sharing any photos or information that you don't want to share or that you wouldn't want shared with the whole world!

● Don't participate in cyberbullying yourself in any way, and do your part to protect other kids. This means not pulling out your phone to video kids fighting—find an adult to break it up instead!

● If someone posts something harmful or private about someone, don't "like" it or share it. If you know someone has created a fake profile and is using it to bully, report it or tell an adult you trust.

Being either the victim of a cyberbully or the cyberbully can have really drastic consequences for a boy's future. Some victims of cyberbullying have been forced to change schools or have had to shut down all their social media accounts, and some cyberbullies have been kicked out of school or have even gone to jail. So please keep yourself safe in the cyberworld.

Give Yourself a Break

The beauty of having the world at your fingertips through a smartphone is that you can reach out to anyone you need to, whenever you need to. The drawback is that the world can also reach you!

Especially as you approach your teen years, when you're building your own social groups outside of your family, social contact becomes more of the focus of your daily life, almost like a job. A fun job, but still a job. If you're on your phone 24/7 and available all the time, that's like working around the clock. Even brain surgeons have days off, right?

Here are a few ways you can take charge of your digital life instead of letting it take charge of you:

● Make sure you have real conversations, not just text conversations with your friends. With texts, you have time to think through every interaction, and exactly how it will be understood and what it says about you, but real-time, real-life conversations are more spontaneous and just as fun!

● Set your phone to airplane mode at night, or use the "do not disturb" function. If you're worried about missing an emergency call, you can set the "do not disturb" to allow incoming calls from your favorites or from the same caller within a short time period, like three minutes.

● Have "screen-free" days once in a while. You deserve to have some personal time. You do not have to be instantly available to everyone you know all the time. Maybe being occasionally unavailable will lend you an air of mystery!

● If you feel like you'd like more screen-free time but have trouble removing yourself from your devices, enlist your parents or other trustworthy adults in your fight. Maybe your house can have a "collect and drop" space where you leave your cell phone or tablet before you go to bed or when you're doing your homework. If you have a big paper to work on and you've already done all the online research, ask the adults at home to serve as your site-blocking software and temporarily change the internet password to keep you on task.

● Did you know that social scientists have done research on how social media impacts how we feel every day, and people who spend the most time on social media are actually the most lonely? The researchers developed that theory that being on social media feels like social interaction, but doesn't have all the qualities of hanging out with people in real life. It's like eating cotton candy when you're really, really hungry instead of sitting down to an actual meal. You can avoid that situation by choosing quality of interaction over quantity of interaction. Instead of belonging to every single social media site, pick one or two that work best for you and limit friends to people you are actually friends with, not people that you have only met once or twice. Use social media to plan for activities in real life, instead of letting it be a substitute for real-life activities.

● Experiment with going to a concert, a movie, or out with friends without taking photos or posting about it on social media. It's a different kind of experience, and you might enjoy it in a different way.

Chapter 7:

THE MESS THAT IS STRESS

Every boy's brain and body are different from every other boy's brain and body, that's a fact. In fact, that's what makes you, well, you! And just like every boy is different, every boy has his very own strengths and weaknesses, or things he does well and things he struggles with. Some of these things you'll notice when doing schoolwork. For example, some boys might be great writers, able to complete 10-page papers with no problem, while others find a two-sentence assignment a huge challenge. You might notice some differences during sports, where there are some boys who are better athletes without even having to try very hard.

All Different Bodies, All Different Brains

Some differences are just part of how a boy's body functions. For example, some boys with ADHD (Attention Deficit Hyperactivity

Disorder) might have trouble sitting still and concentrating. In order to function well in school, these boys might need to take prescription medication to focus and finish their work. If you're one of those boys, it's important to remember there's not something wrong with your brain, your brain just works a little differently.

Sometimes boys have brains that make it hard for them to understand what people mean when they say things, or to understand how friendships and conversations work. Sometimes boys who have brains that work in that specific way are said to have ASD (Autism Spectrum Disorder). They might take medication, they might need to be told things in a certain way, or they might need to be in a classroom that is run in a way that helps their brain work best.

These differences in how different boys' brains and bodies work don't have to be stressful. When the differences do cause stress, it's usually because people in the bigger world haven't spent any time thinking about how they can make sure their part of the world is accessible to people whose brains and bodies might work differently.

For example, a boy might have a body that works a little differently than other kids in his class: instead of walking, he might use a wheelchair to get around. If he lives in a house that is all on one floor with a ramp to the front door, he might not be stressed about using a wheelchair until he shows up for the first day of high school and discovers that there is a huge flight of stairs just to get into the school! Clearly, it's not the wheelchair stressing the boy out; it's the lack of thinking by the people at his school that's causing the stress.

If you've been stressed out by the difference between the way your brain or body works and the way the rest of the world works, remember that everyone has his or her own challenges. No one's brain or body is perfect, no matter how it might appear to an outsider. Every single person on earth struggles with something, so make sure to take the time to learn about other people and know you're not alone.

What should you do if a boy who has a brain or body that might not work exactly like yours has a class with you or rides the bus with you or is in a community group with you? You might feel a little uncertain about how to treat that kid. But there isn't any one way to talk to him because each boy is an individual and each situation is different. Just think about how you'd want to be treated and follow their lead. If you think the boy might want some help with something, ask if you can help, and make sure you listen closely to his answer—don't assume what any boy can or can't do!

You probably know this already, but ignoring or teasing kids who are different than you won't make you (or them) feel good. Every person has feelings, and every boy wants to have friends and be liked. You might find that if you go a little bit out of your way to befriend a kid whose brain or body works differently, that you might be the one who gains the most from the friendship.

Moving

Moving can be a very stressful time in a boy's life. When your parents first tell you that you are going to move, you might be mad. The idea might take some getting used to. After a while, you might want to take some steps that will help you think about how the move might be good for you and for your family. Here are a few first steps:

● Look up your new town online. What is near your house? Is there anything fun there that you couldn't do in your current neighborhood? Google Maps may let you get a 360° view of your new street, neighborhood, and town.

● Look up your new school online and see if you can memorize the names of the teachers and their pictures. That way you can be the new kid who knows all the teachers' names the first time you see them!

● Plan how you want to decorate your new room, and maybe even use some of the more grown-up styles you've been thinking about.

● If you're going to move in the summer, ask if you can join a community sports league, go to activities at the local community center, or visit the local library to meet some kids. That way you don't have to wait until school starts to make friends.

As with most things in life, you'll likely discover that there are both good and bad things about moving. The bad things you've probably already thought about yourself, so here are some good things to keep in mind on this new adventure:

● This is an opportunity to reinvent yourself. No one at your new school knows anything about you. No one knows that you blew the big game, tripped in the hallway, or forgot all your lines in the school play in first grade. You can build yourself a brand-new reputation as the person you want to be.

● You get to make new friends. Choose carefully and you'll probably find friends who will help you navigate all the hard parts of growing up.

● Here's a chance to get closer to your parents and siblings. Since they will be the only ones you know at first, use the time to hang out with them. Play games, explore your neighborhood, and build up your connections to the people who love you most.

Divorce

Although it isn't always as dramatic as it seems on TV, divorce can also be very hard on kids. The most important thing to remember if your parents are getting divorced: it is never, ever, ever (are you listening?) the kids' fault. Divorce is a choice adults make for adult reasons. Even if you were super extra good and never teased your little sister again, or if you were super extra bad and made her life completely miserable, you couldn't cause (or prevent) your parents' divorce.

When parents break up, there is often a lot of shuffling around of kids, and you may have to adjust to having two homes instead of one, or even (later) having a new step parent or step siblings. This can be really difficult, especially at first. If you are having trouble with this, it's important to talk with your parents directly, rather than acting out your feelings with bad behavior. With bad behavior, you might get the attention you want, but it will be negative—not positive—attention.

The Expert Says

Divorce is one of the most stressful things a kid can deal with, but there are ways to make the situation as easy as it can be. Here are a few tips:

● Divorce is more difficult for a family if the parents can't get along at all. Remind your parents that they can have their disagreements when you are not around.

● Accept that some changes will happen. You may have to change schools or even move. You'll get used to your life sooner if you try to look at the positive aspects of it.

● Some families have money problems as parents try to adjust to having two homes and two lives instead of one. You may have to change your spending habits and your expectations of gifts at special occasions.

● Talk to someone. Don't keep your feelings inside—there are people out there who care about you and want to help.

Drugs, Alcohol, and Other Unhealthy Stuff

Hopefully, you are looking at this and thinking, "Why are they talking about this? I am way too young to even think about stuff like that." Unfortunately, that's not true for all boys. In fact, 6 percent of all kids your age say they drink alcohol on a regular basis.

Even if you don't see many people in your life smoking, drinking alcohol, or using illegal drugs, you are still exposed to advertising for alcohol and tobacco products, and you have probably seen movies and TV shows that show people using illegal drugs. So you probably know some things about alcohol and drugs, even if they haven't touched your life directly.

The best place to get information about smoking, drugs, and alcohol is from an adult you trust. They especially need to know if someone asks you to try these things. It's important—but not always easy—to say "no" to drugs.

It's especially hard if there are lots of drugs around you. If this is true for you, talk with the adults that are responsible for taking care of you about changing things in your environment (like where you live, where you go to school, and what adults you are around) to help you stay drug-free. Even

Using marijuana can cause memory loss and learning problems. It can also affect your coordination.

The Expert Says

Lots of boys at this age like to try things that adults consider to be "risky" behavior. If you are looking to gain more independence, keep in mind that there are safe, constructive ways to do it—don't feel like drugs or alcohol are the best way to "test your limits."

if you can't move or change schools, they can help you think up ways to make your environment safer—by changing how you walk to school or finding different activities to be involved in after school, for example.

One of the ways boys are pressured to use drugs is by someone presenting drinking, smoking, or getting high as an adult thing to do. But facing your problems head on and being "in the moment" (instead of being tuned out by illegal substances) is the best way to show how grown-up you are.

Super-Stressed Families

Every family has stress, but some families have much more stress to deal with than others. For example, some families have to cope with having very little money, someone in the family drinking too much or using drugs, homelessness, or living in a neighborhood with a lot of crime.

Sometimes (but not always) situations like this make it hard for the adults in the family to be consistent with discipline and providing for kids' needs, even if they are trying very hard. Sometimes these adults need help so that they can be the kind of parents they want to be.

If you are afraid of someone in your family, aren't getting your basic needs (clothing, food, going to the doctor) met, or your family is super-stressed in some way, it's very important that you talk to someone. Your school guidance counselor or school nurse can be good people to start with. It might be really hard to ask for help, but it is very brave. Often super-stressed families have many strengths, they just need help getting back on track.

Chapter 8:

TO YOUR FUTURE AND BEYOND!

Getting a job after school is a great way to expand your horizons, make some money, and explore and prepare for your future. While you may be too young yet to hold a job in a store or restaurant (two of the more common after-school jobs for teenagers), there are plenty of jobs out there for someone your age. For example, you could mow lawns or shovel snow, you could babysit for your neighbors, you could walk dogs, or you could water plants for people who are on vacation. Often summer camps are able to employee young people starting at age 14 or 15 as counselors in training.

Three of the most important things you will learn from having an after-school job are to take responsibility for the work you do, to do your work the best you can, and how hard you have to work to make money, which will help you appreciate all that your parents have given you. Finally, you'll have money to go to the movies and do the other things you like to do.

Saving, Spending, and Other Hard Decisions

One of the best things about having a small job such as babysitting or mowing lawns is that it makes it possible for you to save some money. Of course, you'll want to put some of the money you make in a special account for when you're ready to go to college or buy your first car, but you can save money for smaller things you need or want as well.

It's easy to spend other people's money; you just walk into the store, pick out what you want, and poof, your parent pulls out their credit card and it's yours. However, when you've taken the time to earn that money yourself, you'll likely have a different feeling about your purchase. When you save for something you want, you

Instead of spending your money on candy and other small stuff, save the money you earn from your job to buy something big you really want. If you save up enough, you'll be the envy of your friends when you buy your first car.

develop an understanding of what it really costs to buy that expensive pair of shoes or electronic gadget. You'll likely discover that you're not just spending money, you're also spending all the work it took to get that money. Is it worth the effort of mowing 25 lawns to get that specific pair of shoes you wanted? The answer depends on your personal experience. You might love and value the shoes even more, or you might decide the shoes were not worth all that!

Exploring Career Options

One of the benefits in getting involved in fun activities outside of regular schoolwork is that you can learn more about what you're good at and what you like to do that has nothing to do with your regularly scheduled classes. You can also meet more adults and get some ideas about jobs you might like to consider for a future career.

Besides extracurricular activities, there are lots of other ways to find out about different jobs. If you think you might be interested in, for example, growing tulips for a living, but you live in Arizona and don't know anyone who grows anything but a cactus now and then, try finding a book about the subject, or ask an adult or teacher to help you find some information online. Also, some colleges include career information for younger students on their websites.

Even if you don't have any career ideas floating around in your head at this point, don't worry. While it's helpful to be thinking about what talents you have and what you can be involved in that will nurture those talents, doing well in school and participating in extracurricular activities is a good start.

It's great to have a certain idea about what you would like to do for work when you get older, but it's also OK to change your mind a lot! There are lots of adults who still aren't sure what they want to be when they grow up!

I can do this!

A college graduate can be expected to earn more than a million dollars more over the course of his life than someone with just a high school diploma.

College, Here I Come (Well, in a Few Years)

You might already be thinking about college, or you might not yet. It's still early, so try and keep your mind open to all the possibilities. Even if no one in your family has been to college, or your family doesn't have a lot of money, it is still possible for you to get a higher education. There are a lot of options—such as scholarships and other types of financial aid—to help you get a higher education. You can also spend your first two years at a community college, which is usually much less expensive than going to a private, four-year school. While college isn't for everyone, going to college can open your eyes to some of the less obvious careers out there. Plus, a good education can help you not only get a job that pays more money, but also to have many more jobs to choose from.

However, a college degree is not the only way to get a job you enjoy. There are some jobs that require specialized training, but not college. Some jobs (such as being a plumber) require you to complete an apprenticeship. An apprenticeship is where you spend time learning from an experienced person in that profession, but not in a formal classroom setting. Generally, jobs that require apprenticeships let you use your body more than an office-type job (like being an accountant or writer). If you are the type of boy who likes to be outside a lot or likes to use his hands to build or fix things, you might want to investigate the types of jobs you can learn through hands-on training. Your adult self will thank you for taking the time to explore all the post–high school opportunities available to you before making a decision that has the power to affect the rest of your life.

BOYS SAY:

I ALWAYS THOUGHT I WANTED TO BE A LAWYER...UNTIL I GOT TO COLLEGE, THAT IS. THEN I HAD THE CHANCE TO TAKE A CLASS IN DIPLOMACY AND I DECIDED I WANTED TO WORK FOR THE AMERICAN EMBASSY. I DIDN'T EVEN KNOW THAT JOB EXISTED WHEN I WAS IN HIGH SCHOOL!

-William, age 21

Conclusion

You are just getting to know yourself in these years and you are going to find out you have many amazing qualities. You are different than anyone else on the planet, and it's this uniqueness (and not your big muscles or acting tough) that puts you on the road to being a real man.

Some men like to watch sports and some men like to play sports. Some men hate sports and would rather spend their time on woodworking projects or playing the guitar. Some men think flowers are stinky and some men love to spend time arranging them. Some men love hunting and some men are vegetarians. None of these men are wrong.

Respect the way you are inside and say good things to yourself. Try to find and be around people who appreciate you and what you have to give. You are growing now, and you have more growing to do, but you are on your way to becoming a strong and caring force in the world around you.

RESOURCES AND FURTHER READING

Books

Feed Your Head: Some Excellent Stuff on Being Yourself

By Earl Hipp

(Hazelden, 1991)

This is an older book, but it has a ton of helpful information about resisting peer pressure.

Our Boys Speak: Adolescent Boys Write About Their Inner Lives

By John Nikkah

(St Martins, 2000)

This book is made up of letters and essays written by young boys. It is broken up into sections by topics like siblings, peer pressure, depression, and school violence. You might find it interesting how many other boys are having feelings and struggles just like yours!

Websites

Name of Website: Preteen Health Talk

Where is it? http://www.pamf.org/preteen/

Who runs it? The Palo Alto Medical Foundation

Lots of information about your changing body can be found here. Also includes sections on your feelings, growing up, and sharing. Another unique feature of this site is that it includes books and movies reviewed by both kids and parents! Includes a special educational resource for parents and teachers about bullying prevention.

Name of Website: BAM! Body and Mind

Where is it? http://www.cdc.gov/bam/

Who runs it? Department of Health and Human Services

This is a huge site that includes information about diseases, food and nutrition, stress, family matters, and conflict resolution (getting along). Also includes games and quizzes and really fun interactive stuff like create your own activity calendar, an interactive game that tests your bully smarts, and a stress-o-meter quiz.

Meet the Contributors

Kelli Dunham is a nurse, stand-up comic, and author of *The Girl's Body Book*, *How to Survive and Maybe Even Love Nursing School* and *How to Survive and Maybe Even Love Your Life as a Nurse.* She has worked as a primary care and home visiting nurse with first-time new moms. She has lived in Port-au-Prince, Haiti, Ohio, Oklahoma, Florida, Portland, Oregon, New York, and on a houseboat in Philadelphia. In her spare time she likes to read and skateboard, and she would really, really like to learn to play the banjo.

Steve Bjorkman has illustrated more than 70 books for children, including picture books such as *Good Night, Little One*, easy readers such as *Thanksgiving Is…*, and series such as *Mama Rex and T.* Steve is also well known for illustrating greeting cards. More than 100 million of his greeting cards for Recycled Paper Greetings have been sold.

Robert Anastas is an educator, author, lecturer, counselor, and the founder of SADD (Students Against Driving Drunk) and the Check in to a Winning Life programs. He received the Massachusetts Teacher of the Year award and the United States Department of Health and Human Services Distinguished Service Award and was a member of the Board of Directors of the National Commission for the Prevention of Alcoholism and Drug Dependency. Anastas has traveled hundreds of thousands of miles throughout North America, Europe, and Asia speaking to more than two million students, educators, and parents about issues relating to alcohol and drug abuse, teen drinking and driving, and parent-child communication.

Index

MY BIG IDEAS

MY GREATEST DREAMS

About Applesauce Press

Good ideas ripen with time. From seed to harvest, Applesauce Press creates books with beautiful designs, creative formats, and kid-friendly information. Like our parent company, Cider Mill Press Book Publishers, our press bears fruit twice a year, publishing a new crop of titles each spring and fall.

"Where Good Books Are Ready for Press"

Visit us on the web at

www.cidermillpress.com

or write to us at

12 Spring Street, PO Box 454

Kennebunkport, Maine 04046